ROCK'N'ROLL
Record Breakers

ROCK'N'ROLL
Record Breakers

THE BIGGEST, THE BADDEST AND THE
BEST GROUPS OF ALL TIME

David McCarthy and Michael Horsham

Additional Research by Edward Dyja

CHARTWELL
BOOKS. INC.

A QUINTET BOOK

Published by Chartwell Books
A Division of Book Sales, Inc.
110 Enterprise Avenue
Secaucus, New Jersey 07094

ISBN 1-55521-776-1

This book was designed and produced by
Quintet Publishing Limited
6 Blundell Street
London N7 9BH

Creative Director: Richard Dewing
Designer: Stuart Walden
Project Editor and Picture Researcher:
Damian Thompson
Editor: Rosemary E. Booton

Typeset in Great Britain by
Central Southern Typesetters, Eastbourne
Manufactured by
Bright Arts (Singapore) Pte Ltd
Printed in Singapore by
Star Standard Industries Private Ltd

CONTENTS

LEFT: The jet-black hair, sunglasses and Gretch guitar became an iconic image of Roy Orbison in the early sixties.

INTRODUCTION

At the awkward age of "thirtysomething" rock music finds itself successful, established and at the centre of a money-spinning industry that spans the globe. Since the late 1950s the world has witnessed the inexorable growth of sales of popular music underpinned by simultaneous explosion in the access to, and availability of, musical media and technology. The means to make and listen to popular music has gradually moved the industry into the public domain; there are few places now left on earth where the presence of some form of rock, pop, or rock 'n' roll has not made a qualitative difference to human life.

The secret of the longevity of rock music lies in its ability to effect radical changes in its content while remaining instantly recognizable as rock. The music, attitude and image associated with the most successful artists of any one year, help to set and reflect the fashions, mood and tone of the times. What is then current is usually superseded by something "brand new" or even revivalist and the cycle of generation and replacement begins again. Every so often, the primitive roots of the musical form recur and are presented to the public, who seize upon, say, the three chord trick as "new", and the regenerative process starts once more.

In the course of its relatively brief history, rock has witnessed many changes, not least in the methods of musical reproduction employed by the industry. The original, radio-fuelled rock 'n' roll boom used first the 78rpm and then the 45rpm single, backed up by the 33.33rpm album as its major formats. In the late fifties and early sixties single record sales in the millions were a regular occurrence – resulting in the setting of many sales records at the time. Towards the end of the sixties came a rise in the popularity of the album, with a more serious view taken of the cultural impact and importance of rock's major players.

The huge stadium bands of the seventies saw vast tours and attendances become the norm, and the same decade saw the first rumblings of the threat to the supremacy of the vinyl record with the arrival of the CC (Compact Cassette). Walkman technology, together with the development of state-of-the-art ICE (In Car Entertainment) systems, played no small part in the success of the format.

The arrival of the CD (Compact Disc) in the eighties signalled the death knell for vinyl as a viable medium, with many releases appearing only on CC or CD and some on the very latest of formats, Digital Audio Tape or DAT. The emergence of these new formats, with their superb sound reproductive qualities, means that sales figures for albums are constantly shifting as collectors and fans alike replace their worn vinyl records with CD versions and enjoy hearing details they never noticed before on their favourite records.

For this reason, this book of records is not simply a list of sales figures, although where appropriate, this information does appear; rather, this is an, at times, oblique view of the world of rock music, the people and personalities who have contributed and helped to create the music and its mythology over the years. There are many firsts within these pages and there are also a number of categories you may not have thought of, containing the kind of legends, anecdotes and background information invaluable to the true fan. *Rock Music Record Breakers* awaits your pleasure.

David McCarthy
Michael Horsham
1991

· ABBA ·

Few people are aware that as well as being an acronym for the Christian names of the group members, ABBA is also the name of the largest fish cannery operation in Sweden, and Benny Anderson had to negotiate usage of the name with the company. ABBA (Agnetha, Bjorn, Benny and Anni-Frid) first recorded under the title of The Engaged Couples, and their 1971 single "She's My Kind of Girl" sold over 250,000 copies in Japan. After adopting the new name in 1972 they had their first chart-topper all over Europe with "Ring Ring", whose English lyrics were penned by old hand Neil Sedaka. ABBA also hold the distinction of being the only group of any note or lasting worth to win the Eurovision Song Contest, in 1974 with "Waterloo", which hit the top 10 on both sides of the Atlantic.

It was in Australia that ABBA had the most astounding success. After having five singles in the Australian top thirty in the same week in 1976, it was estimated that one in four Australians owned a copy of the group's *Greatest Hits*.

In 1979 the group's album *Voulez Vous* sold over a million copies within a month of its release, and in the same year they were officially recognized as the biggest-selling group in recording history. Appropriately enough ABBA's last UK hit single was "Thank You for the Music".

ABOVE: **Agnetha, Bjorn, Benny and Anna-Frid** first achieved international recognition in 1974 through winning the Eurovision Song Contest.

RIGHT: **An estimated one in four Australians** owned a copy of the group's *Greatest Hits* by the late seventies, and Abba's Antipodean tour formed the basis for their movie.

ADVANCES

A rtists worldwide are continually in search of the elusive recording and publishing deal which will enable them to get their music to the waiting public and then, perhaps more importantly, reap the financial rewards. Over the years, the music business has gained a reputation as a minefield of sharp practice and dodgy dealings in which the managers and recording companies often fare better than their creative charges. Since the late 1960s, however, the more successful artistes have found themselves increasingly in a position to dictate terms to their recording companies.

In 1991 Michael Jackson eclipsed his sister Janet (the previous record-holder) by securing the largest recording contract ever with Sony Corporation. Reputedly worth a staggering $18 million cash advance for the album *Dangerous* and a guaranteed $5 million advance on subsequent projects, the deal also included an extremely favourable royalty rate of $2.08 per unit.

At the other end of the scale James Marshall Hendrix must be a contender for signing for the smallest amount of money. On 15 October 1965 Jimi signed a recording contract with PPX Productions, for which he received an advance of $1 against a paltry one per cent royalty rate. Jimi is reputed to have posted a dollar bill soaked in his own blood to his PPX boss Ed Chaplin only days before his untimely death.

RIGHT: **Michael Jackson backed up his self-proclaimed "king of pop" tag by signing the** most lucrative contract in record company history, with the Sony Corporation in 1991.

BOOTLEGS

The music business, like any other, is based on the principle of supply and demand, and the official releases of favourite artistes are generally not enough to satisfy the appetites of obsessive fans for trivia, minutiae and so-called rare recordings. The mid-1960s first saw the appearance of mass-produced bootleg records. Bob Dylan's controversial shows at London's Royal Albert Hall in 1965, where he played a full electric set backed by The Band, were the first to be exploited fully in this way. Dylan's later recordings with The Band, made at their house "Big Pink" in Woodstock, New York during Dylan's 18-month layoff in 1967, produced the first big-selling, world-wide bootleg in the shape of *Great White Wonder*. Tracks included "The Mighty Quinn" and "This Wheel's on Fire", which were both contemporaneous world-wide hits for other artistes. The recordings eventually saw the light of day as the officially released *The Basement Tapes* in 1975. The album achieved top-10 status in the charts on either side of the Atlantic.

Most major acts have found their material appearing illicitly on street corners and in specialist record shops, with the record companies claiming that this was a siphoning-off of legitimate revenue. There is, however, a case to be made for the suggestion that the bootlegger is providing a much-needed service for the die-hard fan. In 1967, Brian Wilson was working on the follow-up to the Beach Boys hugely successful *Pet Sounds*. The project was proceeding under the working title of *Smile*, with the tracks "Good Vibrations" and "Heroes and Villains" already completed and hinting at the quality of the work underway. One night, while working on a track title "Fire", a drug-befuddled Wilson reputedly became obsessed with what he imagined to be the magical and mystical properties of the song he was recording. As a consequence, he set fire to the tapes and retired to the non-inflammable safety of the legendary sandbox in which he used to write. Capitol salvaged some of the material as a later release, *Smiley Smile*, but it was left to the bootlegger to release the material as *Smile*, which has since become one of the many bootlegs available on CD.

Another kind of bootleg is that which contains material deemed to be unreleasable by the record company. The Rolling Stones "Cocksucker Blues", delivered to Decca in July 1970 as the final fulfilment of their contractual obligations, was deemed to be unsuitable for general consumption. The story is of a "lonesome schoolboy" at loose in London for the first time, and dwells on his thoughts on the nature of his sexual encounters with a policeman. It appeared only as a bootlegged 45 in the late seventies and qualifies as the most explicitly rude unreleased rock record.

In keeping with their record-breaking status in many other areas, the most bootlegged act in the world is, of course, The Beatles. Live recordings such as the earliest performances in Hamburg, the Decca demos, their final performances at Shea Stadium, copies of their fan-club-only Christmas messages, out-takes from studio, film and television appearances, along with completed masters such as the legendary "What's New, Mary Jane?", go to make up a repository of bootlegged work rivalling the official releases in popularity and desirability among the most avid of Beatles fans.

BELOW: **A selection of illegally recorded and distributed albums by Meatloaf, Blondie, Bob Dylan and David Bowie. Do bootlegs siphon off legitimate revenue or provide a much needed service for fans?**

· THE BEATLES ·

With more than 20 years hindsight, it is easy to underestimate the impact of the four lads who shook the world. Their list of achievements includes many firsts, and many record-breaking feats which still stand today.

In terms of record sales the group set a blistering pace which only a few subsequent acts have even come close to equalling. The group's third single "From Me to You" was the first record to top all of the UK singles charts, and also the first of a record-breaking run of 11 consecutive number-one singles. "She Loves You" sold 1.6 million copies and was the biggest UK-selling single until Paul McCartney's "Mull of Kintyre" overtook it in 1977. Their second album *With the Beatles* was the first million-selling album in the UK and, together with their debut album *Please Please Me*, saw The Beatles occupy the number one slot in the album charts for 51 consecutive weeks.

When "I Want To Hold Your Hand" hit the top spot on the singles chart in December 1963, it was the first record to displace another by the same artist,

OPPOSITE, TOP: **Seen here with original drummer Pete Best, the Beatles ditched him, along with their leather-clad image, before signing to Parlophone.**

OPPOSITE, BOTTOM: **Paul McCartney and John Lennon pictured in conversation with US television legend Ed Sullivan during their first Stateside tour in 1964.**

ABOVE: **Plastic Beatles mannikins produced in 1963.**

LEFT: **The US tour, 1964; the Beatles proved themselves masters of the jokey photo-opportunity.**

TRADE MARK OF
THE GRAMOPHONE CO. LTD.

removing "She Loves You" in the process. The only time this was to happen again was when John Lennon posthumously replaced himself performing "Imagine" with his subsequent hit "Woman" in 1981.

In the US, in 1964, "I Want to Hold Your Hand" was the fastest-ever million seller recorded by a UK artist. In April of that year the group had a record 14 singles in the US chart. Back in the UK, in 1964, "Can't Buy Me Love" accrued the biggest-ever advance orders for a single with over one million copies.

In 1965, The Beatles became the first group ever to have their achievements officially recognized by the Establishment, when they were awarded MBEs by the then British Prime Minister, Harold Wilson. They went to Buckingham Palace in October of that year to receive their medals from Queen Elizabeth II.

In 1967, with the release of "Sergeant Pepper's Lonely Hearts Club Band" came the first simultaneous release of an

TOP: The Beatles became the first group to be honoured by the British Establishment, when wily UK Prime Minister Harold Wilson awarded them MBEs for services to the export industry.

ABOVE: George Harrison, Stu Sutcliffe and John Lennon in Hamburg, during the time when Sutcliffe played bass in an early five-strong Beatles line-up.

album in America and Britain. The set was also the first to feature the entire lyrics of the songs printed on the reverse of the gatefold sleeve.

In September 1968, the first release on The Beatles' new label, Apple Records, was "Hey Jude". It became the longest-playing continuous number-one single on both sides of the Atlantic, lasting a lengthy seven minutes and 10 seconds.

In 1970, the band's last single release "Let It Be" entered the American singles charts at number six, the highest new entry ever. Finally, and as a testament to The Beatles out-of-this-world contribution to music, four asteroids, previously known as 4147-4150, received new names in 1990; they are now known as Lennon, McCartney, Harrison and, appropriately enough, Starr.

Beatles merchandising reached a peak in the mid sixties – guitar and Beatle badges (above) and a yellow submarine (below).

CRASHES

The nature of the job of a rock 'n' roller means that inordinate amounts of time are spent on the road between venues in cities often miles apart. Touring is as much a part of the rock 'n' roll machine as guitars and drum kits, recording and after-show parties. Constant travel leaves the musicians and back-up teams involved in producing rock shows statistically vulnerable to accidents, with the result that many rockers have died in the execution of their duties.

On 2 February 1959, The Big Bopper, Richie Valens and Buddy Holly unwillingly and tragically participated in the first rock 'n' roll air disaster. Halfway through their "Winter Dance Party" package tour, the three chart-topping chums, tired of bus travel and the hardships of the road, decided to fly to the next date at Moorehead, Minnesota. Minutes after take-off in bad weather their Beechcraft Bonanza crashed, killing all on board. It was the first fatal, multiple rock 'n' roll crash, but by no means the last.

The shocking deaths resulted in a morbid fear of flying in the young Eddie Cochran, but this didn't stop him from jetting all the way across the Atlantic for a UK tour with fellow rocker Gene Vincent. On 17 April 1960, in a bid to avoid the tedium of travel on British Rail, Cochran, his girlfriend Sharon Sheeley and Vincent drove along the A4 to London in a rented Ford Consul. The car swerved out of control and hit a lamp-post on a bend near Chippenham in Wiltshire. Vincent suffered a broken collarbone, but Cochran died in hospital after being hurled through the windscreen.

Southern boogie-merchants Lynyrd Skynyrd suffered a tragic accident on 20 October 1977, when their Corvair 240 aircraft crashed into a swamp on the way to a show at Louisiana University. There were four deaths: Ronnie van Zant, Steve Gaines, back-up singer Cassie Gaines and manager Dean Kilpatrick. Four members of the band were severely injured, but later recovered. Many commentators have noted that the band's next scheduled album release eerily featured a cover of Skynyrd surrounded by ferocious fire. The title of the set was even more ironic – *Street Survivors*.

ABOVE: **On the way from a concert at Louisiana University, Lynyrd Skynyrd lost three members and their manager in a plane crash in 1977.**

RIGHT: **The tangled wreckage of a Beechcraft Bonanza airplane marks the spot where Buddy Holly, Richie Valens and the Big Bopper died.**

CENSORSHIP

Rock music has always pushed the boundaries of good taste and of what is acceptable to the general public and the corporations in control of marketing and production. For the young in mid-fifties America there was an inherent danger and rebellion in rock 'n' roll which served to distance the newly defined teenager from their increasingly estranged elders. The last 30 years have seen rock become the battlefield for arguments over morality, sexuality, politics and freedom of expression.

After a scorching ad-libbed coda to a performance of "Hound Dog" on American national television in June 1956, Elvis Presley was castigated for the blatant sexuality of his hip-wiggling, baggy-trousered grinding to the slowed-down beat. Shot full-length and surrounded by his sweating band, Presley shocked and stunned the Bible Belt, NBC executives and parents across the nation. Forced to apologize and made to sing "Hound Dog" in white tie and tails after being introduced as "the new Elvis Presley" by Steve Allen, Elvis was then actively censored by the NBC network and other television stations. Orders were carried out only to film Elvis from the waist up and Ed Sullivan initially refused to have him on his show. However for Presley and his machiavellian manager, Tom Parker, the launch of the young demi-god-to-be had gone exceedingly well.

LEFT: **James Dean has become an icon to more than one generation of disaffected teenagers.**

RIGHT: **Elvis Presley's "bumping and grinding" hips caused outrage on early television appearances. This led to the first instances of censorship in rock and roll, when cameramen were directed to shoot him from the waist up only.**

ABOVE: **In 1964 Mick Jagger was forced to change the lyrics of "Let's Spend the Night Together" for the Ed Sullivan Show.**

cial clout of a major network, Mick Jagger agreed to change the offending line, resulting in an embarrassed rubber-lipped rendition of "Let's spend *some time* together". As bassist Bill Wyman said some years later, "even the Stones compromised sometimes".

Some groups singularly refused to compromise their art for the lure of easy money. Instead, they flew further in the face of the moral majority and found, to their delight, that easy money was still the result. The Doors' Jim Morrison made a point of singing the supposedly drug-inspired lyric of "Light My Fire" on national television and went on to outrage police and the authorities further and invited the use of the censors' scissors by exposing himself on stage. Numerous arrests – a form of civic censorship – failed to prevent and perhaps even assisted the success of the band and the rise of the singer to cult status.

More recently, arch purveyors of steamy sexuality such as Madonna and American rappers 2LiveCrew, have found themselves on the receiving end of a rigidly enforced moral backlash. Madonna was threatened with arrest during her Blonde Ambition Tour in 1990, when the show reached Toronto, Canada. The police were called to prevent Ms Ciccone from performing the infamous masturbatory sequence during her teen-favourite anthem "Like A Virgin". Refusing to bow to the pressure of the authorities, and steadfastly sticking to her right to communicate her ideas through the performance of her art, Madonna went right ahead and delivered the full choreography to the slowed-down pop classic. Pointy-breasted, Gaultier-clad men caressed the singer's body as she lay across a harem-style bed, and the audience loved it. After witnessing the

The American television networks were often the arena for major confrontations between the moral majority and the teenage minority. After a riotous performance in 1964, Ed Sullivan had stated that he never again would allow the Rolling Stones to appear on his ratings-topping CBS show. Three years later, however, the group were booked to perform a version of their current single "Let's Spend the Night Together". In spite of the much-vaunted permissiveness of the times, the lyric of the song was deemed unsuitable for the youth of America. Bowed by the commer-

ABOVE: **"We stock Sex Pistols."** The refusal of some record stores to sell *Never Mind the Bollocks,* as well as bans on commercial radio, turned into a publicity gift for the group.

LEFT: **Rappers 2LiveCrew found themselves at the forefront of the censorship debate in the US with their sexually explicit lyrics.**

spectacle, the Toronto police declined to arrest the star on the grounds of obscenity, having found little of offence in the content of the performance. Furthermore, the audience had not been outraged, but had been entertained, vindicating Madonna's belief in her own talents.

But pop performers have found themselves increasingly under the watchful gaze of the moral majority, who seek to lay the blame for many of society's ills at the door of popular music and its makers. The emergence of Tipper Gore and the equally vociferous Washington Wives pressure group has led to the widespread use of warning stickers on the albums of artistes in America. Perversely, the use of stickers to proclaim the adult content of a number of records on the racks of US record stores has had precisely the opposite effect to that which was intended.

But concern over the perceived power of rock music to corrupt and adversely influence the young has not been confined to the USA and Canada. In 1978, the old

Anglo-Saxon word "bollocks" became the centrepiece of a trial involving the original punk rockers, The Sex Pistols. Their album, *Never Mind The Bollocks Here's The Sex Pistols,* had attracted the kind of attention for which the group had become famous, merely on the strength of its title. The album had to be withdrawn from sale while the British legal system decided whether "bollocks" was an offensive word. (It decided not.) The previous year's single, "God Save The Queen", with its collage of Elizabeth II wearing a safety-pin through her lip, was banned from national daytime radio in the UK and was not sold by the major record retailers. However, it still managed to sell 150,000 copies within five days of its release. In June 1977, the record went to number two in the UK singles charts behind Rod Stewart's "I Don't Want To Talk About It", amid claims that the Pistols' Silver Jubilee offering was actually outselling Rod's sentimental ballad, although this has not actually been proved.

· THE CLASH ·

S i d e 1

JANIE JONES
REMOTE CONTROL
I'M SO BORED WITH THE U.S.A.
WHITE RIOT
HATE & WAR
WHAT'S MY NAME*
DENY
LONDON'S BURNING

<u>THE CLASH</u>   Mick Jones   - guitar, vocals
                 Joe Strummer - guitar, vocals
                 Paul Simonon - bass guitar
                 Tory Crimes - drums

All songs written by Strummer/Jones
except* Strummer/Jones/K.Levine and ** Murvin/Perry.

Photographs: Front Cover - Kate Simon; Back Cover - Rocco Maca

The Clash were one of the three major punk groups to emerge from the explosion of new music in the late seventies in the UK. Together with The Sex Pistols and The Jam, The Clash helped to define a particular music, played with a particular attitude. They were, however, the only group to go on to make any considerable impact in commercial terms in the world arena.

Their first eponymous album was deemed to be too raw, crude and angry for American release when it appeared in 1977. CBS's reticence proved to be the key to the band's entry into the record books, when *The Clash* became the biggest-selling import album to America ever, shipping well over 100,000 copies.

Their third album, the double *London Calling,* was voted Best Album of the Eighties by *Rolling Stone* magazine in their round-up of the decade. Unfortunately, the fact that the record was released in 1979 seemed to escape their attention.

After accompanying The Who on their farewell tour of American stadia in 1982, The Clash album *Combat Rock* went on to become their biggest US success, entering the top 10 and selling over 1 million copies.

LEFT: The Clash hold the record for the biggest-selling import album to the USA, with 100,000 copies of their self-titled debut.

BELOW: Joe Strummer of the Clash auditions for Lightning Strike.

DRUMMERS

What do you call someone who hangs around with musicians? Answer – a drummer! If you can't sing and haven't got 10 years to learn how to play a proper instrument, but still want to be in a band, ask yourself one simple question: are you any good at hitting things? If the answer is yes, perhaps you should buy yourself a drum kit, or alternatively, hit someone who already owns one and then take theirs.

John Bonham, whose record-breaking drum solos formed the centrepiece of many a Led Zeppelin live ordeal by jamming, was the first to dispense altogether with drumsticks. Bonzo, as he was affectionately called, used his bare hands in an unashamed display of caveman-like expressivity.

Cozy Powell is honoured with the distinction of having the only hit record featuring solely drums, or a drum solo, in "Dance with the Devil" with its characteristic flum-flum-flum-flum-flum-fler-digger-digger rhythm.

Phil Collins drums with extreme rhythmic precision and so is regarded as one of the world's better drummers. His record-breaking activities are too numerous to mention here, but careful perusal of this book will reveal his name cropping up again and again.

Pete Townshend of The Who claimed a record on behalf of his dead fellow band member Keith "The Loon" Moon, when he said, "(Keith) was the most spontaneous and unpredictable drummer in rock". Somewhat predictably, Moon died young after pursuing a legendary hedonistic rock 'n' roll lifestyle.

ABOVE LEFT: **John Bonham left the Yardbirds in 1969 to join the now legendary Led Zeppelin.**

FAR LEFT: **Phil Collins was widely recognized as one of the finest rock drummers in the world before his solo-singer/ songwriter success.**

LEFT: **Keith Moon was called "the most spontaneous and inspired drummer in rock" by fellow Who member Pete Townshend.**

DRUGS

In keeping with the role of rock 'n' roll as a method of rebellion, drugs have always played an integral part in it, with the most popular drugs varying from era to era. Taking their cue from the lifestyle of jazz musicians in pre- and post-war America, many early rockers in the fifties and sixties used amphetamines or "speed" to boost and maintain the raw energy needed both for intensive recording sessions and the gruelling existence of life on the road.

Drugs first became a focus for the emerging transatlantic pop counter-culture of the sixties when Dylan met The Beatles in a New York hotel in 1964. This meeting of like-minded musicians saw Dylan introduce The Beatles to the aromatic delights of marijuana. Tellingly, when Bob offered the band one of his "cigarettes", the more worldly Ringo tried it first before the other three would join in.

The only drug to start a whole sub-culture of its own was LSD. By 1967 it was established as the heart of a

BELOW: **The Beatles seen here some years after being introduced to Dylan's friend Mary Jane.**

ABOVE: **The influence of LSD on the counter-culture of the mid sixties provided a colourful backdrop for the times.**

scene based around the San Fransisco Bay area, with the term "psychedelic" being coined to cover all aspects of the consciousness-expanding "hippy" movement. The "Summer of Love" began in Haight-Ashbury fuelled by acid, and ended the world over when the drug-fuelled dream began to sour.

Heroin, another overhang of the jazz era, claimed the lives of many stars towards the end of the sixties and during the early seventies. Jimi Hendrix and Janis Joplin died within three weeks of each other in 1970, and the highly-publicised addictions of Clapton and Townshend together with John Lennon's own autobiographical song "Cold Turkey", helped to strip away any glamour still clinging to the image of the evil opiate.

In the mid-seventies the shabby mantle previously worn by now-deceased, drugged-out rockers was worn by the so-called "toxic twins" Joe Perry and Steve Tyler of proto-stadium rockers Aerosmith. The band cleaned up their act in the eighties to the extent that while on tour with support group Guns 'n' Roses the contract was rumoured to have contained a clause stating that the support group were to limit their chemical abuse to the confines of their dressing-rooms. Apparently, this was in order not to tempt the headliners into a repeat of their former behaviour.

By the mid-eighties designer-drug MDMA, better known as Ecstacy, E or Uncle Ernie (taken from a character in The Who's Rock Opera *Tommy*), was the most popular drug. But the role of cocaine in the higher echelons of the rock hierarchy is also not insignificant, causing already large egos to inflate still further.

LEFT: **The ultimately self-destructive talents of Janis Joplin led to a fatal dabbling with heroin – she died of an overdose on 4 October 1970 in Hollywood.**

BELOW AND OPPOSITE: **Guns 'n' Roses battled it out with stadium rockers Aerosmith in an attempt to become the most hedonistic rock and roll band in the world.**

· DYLAN ·

ABOVE: **Bob Dylan and Joan Baez outside the Savoy Hotel in London, May 1965.**

of "Blowin' in the Wind" in 1963 and followed it into the charts with another Dylan cover "Don't Think Twice It's Alright". Dylan's first number one in the States was "Mr Tambourine Man", a song taken to the top by The Byrds in 1965. Later that year, other acts to take Dylan songs into the charts included The Turtles, Cher, Joan Baez and Manfred Mann. The latter group also had a world-wide hit in 1967 with a track taken from the unreleased *Great White Wonder,* as did Julie Driscoll and Brian Auger. The following year, Jimi Hendrix covered "All Along the Watchtower", another world-wide hit.

Dylan also holds the record for the creation of, and appearance in, all-star backing groups. It was a trend he started when he used Al Kooper and Paul Butterfield in his band, who were to render the first rock treatment of Dylan material on the LP *Bringing It All Back Home,* in 1965. Dylan was subsequently backed by The Band, a group who were to attain critical and public acclaim in their own right.

In the seventies Dylan put together his Rolling Thunder Revue featuring, among others, Roger McGuinn, Joan Baez, Joni Mitchell, Mick Ronson and Allen Ginsberg. The next decade saw Dylan's albums feature musicians of the calibre of Eric Clapton, Mark Knopfler, Jerry Garcia, ex-Pistol Steve Jones, Clash bassist Paul Simenon and Rolling Stone Ron Wood. Woody also joined with fellow-Stone Keith Richards to back Dylan for his closing numbers at Live Aid.

Other star-studded Dylan spectaculars of the eighties saw Dylan backed by Tom Petty's Heartbreakers and the "father of folk-rock" treading the boards with the Grateful Dead. Dylan rounded off the decade in true supergroup style by becoming part of the superstar-laden outfit, The Traveling Wilburys.

Born Robert Allan Zimmerman in 1941, Bob Dylan first saw success as a songwriter whose work was taken to a wider public by other artistes. Peter, Paul and Mary sold over a million copies

ABOVE: **George Harrison and Dylan.**

ABOVE RIGHT: **Tom Petty's Heartbreakers toured with Dylan in the eighties.**

BELOW: **Bruce Springsteen, Bob Dylan and Mick Jagger – yet another Dylan-inspired gathering of rock dinosaurs.**

BELOW RIGHT: **The world's most super supergroup – Roy Orbison, Jeff Lynne, Bob Dylan, Tom Petty and George Harrison: the Traveling Wilburys.**

ELECTRIC GUITAR

Although electrically amplified guitars had been around since the mid-1930s it was the advent of the solid-bodied guitar which was to transform the sound of popular music. In 1947, Paul Bigsby perfected a prototype of a solid-bodied electric guitar but this innovation was swiftly eclipsed by the introduction of Leo Fender's Broadcaster, which became widely available the following year. It was the first solely electric guitar designed to be used only with an amplifier. Renamed the Telecaster in 1950, this guitar went on to become one of the most distinctive-sounding and popular models in the world.

Les Paul, broken-armed guitar maestro of the big band era, struck a deal with the Gibson guitar manufacturing company leading to the introduction of the Gold Top Les Paul Standard in 1952. Although a groundbreaking and popular guitar, it was not until the mid-1960s that it was to rise to world-wide pre-eminence through its use by white blues-influenced guitarists.

Leo Fender claims yet another instrumental record in his invention of the electric bass guitar in 1951 when he introduced the Precision Bass. "Fender Bass" became a generic term after Monk Montgomery, bassist with Lionel Hampton, was the first to play it.

ABOVE: **Les Paul, designer of the mass-produced Gibson guitar that bears his name.**

ENDING

Towards the run-off of any of your traditionally recorded vinyl albums and singles you will find what musicians refer to as "the ending". The first record released on The Beatles' own label Apple Records, was "Hey Jude", in 1968. Working on the premise of value for money, they released a characteristically snappy three-minute pop song and tacked on a four-minute ending – the longest fade commercially released on a single.

RIGHT: **The first release on the Beatles' own label Apple was "Hey Jude" in 1967, famous for its four-minute coda.**

EUROVISION

The Eurovision Song Contest began in 1956 as a pioneering live television music link-up between European nations. Great Britain was not to participate until the following year, but since then has appeared with a monotonous regularity which belies the wealth of musical talent that has emerged from the UK. Middle-of-the-road pop perennials Lulu and Cliff Richard both contributed winning entries, but it was not until ABBA's barnstorming victory in 1974, with "Waterloo", that a major pop powerhouse was to break internationally as a result of winning a song contest.

The result of the contest is decided by a panel of judges sited in each of the participating countries. These judges award each entry points on the strength of the song. The first nation ever to compete in the contest and, at the end of the lengthy judging process, to emerge with a legendary "nul points" was Norway in 1972, who even managed to make their record unassailable by repetition of it the very next year.

· ELVIS ·

Elvis Presley deserves his place in the record books if only for the fact that he was the first person successfully to meld two distinct cultures, in taking black music into the homes and lives of the moneyed white public. Needless to say, Presley also broke other records in the course of his career.

When he signed to RCA Records in 1955, the company paid the largest advance to date when it handed over a cool $35,000 to Sam Phillips of Sun Records, and a further $5,000 to Presley himself. The singer's success in the US charts attained record-breaking status in 1956 when "Hound Dog" and "Don't Be Cruel" held the top two singles placings for seven weeks. The sales of the record on which these two songs appeared exceeded five million copies in the US alone. Presley's Midas touch was also seen to work when the star first became involved in Hollywood. His debut motion picture *Love Me Tender*

recouped its million dollar budget in just over a week. A further record was broken when 550 prints of the film were sent out to theatres all over the States.

In 1957 Presley had a record eight releases in the UK singles chart at the same time, and he remains the artist with the most weeks at number one to this day. Another ground-breaking feat was achieved when "Jailhouse Rock" became the first single ever to enter the charts at number one.

Elvis also holds the strange record of being the most famous teenager ever to be drafted into the US Army. While stationed at Friedberg, near Hamburg in Germany, he became the only US Army corporal to buy his own mansion just outside the base.
Presley's biggest-selling single world-wide was "It's Now Or Never", released in 1960, shifting 20 million copies. He achieved another first in 1969 when he became the first major performer of the

rock 'n' roll years to stage a fully fledged comeback. An eight-year absence from live work had led to a corresponding drop in the number of hit records. Presley staged his comeback with characteristic flair, returning to centre stage in the 1969 television special simply called "Elvis". Clad in a skin-tight black leather jumpsuit, Elvis was surrounded by musicians from his past, and the subsequent jam session featuring several rock standards saw Elvis once more in his rightful position as the King of Rock 'n' Roll. He went on to bigger and more flamboyant success with his live television spectacular "Aloha From Hawaii" in 1973, drawing what was then the largest television audience for a single show, with an estimated one billion viewers. Elvis' final claim to fame is that he remains the only rock star to have been publically inaugurated by President Nixon as an agent for the FBI. Or was he?

LEFT: **The King reclaimed his crown in 1969, with a return to a rock-based collection of songs. His following proved just as large when he came out of retirement.**

OPPOSITE: **Elvis holds the record for most weeks spent at the top of the UK singles chart – 73! "Jailhouse Rock" is the first record ever to enter the singles chart at number one.**

FAILURE

ven an act as consistently successful as The Beatles during the 1960s found that they had to face the grim spectre of failure. After "Please Please Me" hit the number-one slot in May 1963, all 10 subsequent singles went to the same august position until, in 1967, "Penny Lane/Strawberry Fields" only managed to climb to number two. Some failure!

Real failure can be found in such debacles as the saga of Brinsley Schwarz, a band of British pub rockers, who for a short period in the early seventies (about two weeks) were heralded as the "next big thing". Flown out with a planeload of journalists to witness shows at the Filmore East, New York, the trip is generally regarded to have been one of rock's most prominent unmitigated promotional disasters. The band broke up shortly afterwards.

ABOVE AND BELOW: **UK pub rockers Brinsley Schwarz are known for failing to become well known! Group members Dave Edmonds and Nick Lowe went on to** **resurrect their careers as singer/songwriters.**

FAMILIES

Many famous record labels have been based on familial links. The first and most successful of these in terms of rock music was Chess (originally founded as Aristocrat Records in 1947), which from the late forties released a string of classic recordings by the likes of Muddy Waters, Howlin' Wolf and Little Walter. The label, founded by Polish immigrant brothers Leonard and Phil Chess, continued its ground-breaking success in the 1950s with pioneering releases by the progenitor of rock 'n' roll himself, Chuck Berry.

A song called "Money" was recorded by Barret Strong in the Chess studios. It was written by a Detroit car-production worker called Berry Gordy Jr. The single first appeared on Anna Records, a label owned by Gordy's sister, but with a borrowed $600 he swiftly re-

ABOVE: **Major Motown motivator Smokey Robinson (left), seen here with his Miracles. They were discovered by "Reet Petite" compose Berry Gordy Jr in 1957.**

ABOVE: **The understated image of the Jackson 5 helped them to form the basis of the success of Motown's third wave.**

BELOW: **The clean-cut Everly brothers Don and Phil. Their million-seller "Bye Bye Love" was the foundation for a legendary career.**

released it on his own Tamla Records. It was a sizeable hit and prefigured the first million seller on the label, "Shop Around" by The Miracles. This band featured Smokey Robinson, who went on to play a major role in the Motown success story, writing for and producing a considerable number of Gordy's stable of talented young black artists.

Tamla Motown went on to fulfil Berry Gordy's idea of creating a major recording label with a distinctly black identity but a universal appeal. Indeed, Stevie Wonder's "Fingertips Pt2" was the first record to feature simultaneously in the R 'n' B charts and the Billboard Top 100. It also has the distinction of being the first live recording ever to have topped the US charts. In the midst of this unprecedented success the company was still run along the lines of a close-knit family unit, operating from three connected houses on Grand West Boulevard, Detroit which contained the offices, recording studios and production facilities.

The family ethic perhaps saw its ultimate expression in the success of The Jackson Five. Having been suggested to Gordy by Diana Ross, who had witnessed the brothers in action in their hometown of Gary, Indiana, the band was signed on a long-term production and development deal resulting in their first chart success with "I Want You Back". The group went on to have three number ones with their first three releases, the first time this had been achieved in the US.

The first example of a successful family rock act was The Everly Brothers. Don and Phil began their perform-

ABOVE: **Dennis, Brian and Carl Wilson (back row, except second from right) formed the nucleus of the Beach Boys. The four principal themes of their early songs were surfing, girls, cars and . . . more girls.**

ing career as The Everly Family with their parents Ike and Margaret. It soon became apparent to the elder Everlys that the boys had a far greater chance for success if they struck out on their own. Their first million seller "Bye Bye Love" proved them right.

The Beach Boys took the family idea a stage further. With the guidance of their father Mr Wilson Snr,

brothers Brian, Dennis and Carl were joined with cousin Al Jardine to form the nucleus of the close-harmonizing, clean-cut, crew-cut, collegiate, surfing songsters.

Other "families" who drew upon the attraction of familial status but who were in no way related include The Righteous Brothers, The Walker Brothers, The Mamas and The Papas and, of course, Family.

· FLEETWOOD MAC ·

The Macs hold the record for appearing in more guises and with more personnel changes than any other group while retaining the same name. In a long career which began in 1967 and continues today, the central core of the group, Mick Fleetwood, has not changed but other musicians have come and gone. Most notable of these is Peter Green. Originally a prime mover in the band, Green's switch from Judaism to Christianity caused the first split in what had become an extraordinarily successful act, with hits such as the plaintive "Man of the World" and the instrumental "Albatross".

Unable to cope with the pressure of stardom, Green took to appearing in a long white robe for performances and shortly after, in 1970, quit the band. It was at this point that Christine McVie joined the band. The line-up changed again the following year when one of the original guitarists with the band, Jeremy Spencer, left while on tour in the US. Having told the group that he was just slipping out of their LA hotel "to get some newspapers" he was not seen again for two years.

By 1974, Fleetwood Mac were in their tenth incarnation in seven years when the line-up stabilized for a long enough period to make them one of the biggest-selling acts of the seventies with the albums *Fleetwood Mac* and *Rumours*. The latter was to sell over 15 million units, spending 400 weeks on the UK chart and 130 on the US equivalent.

In 1979, the end of a romantically, financially and personally tumultuous decade for Fleetwood Mac, came the release of the double album *Tusk,* featuring the single of the same name which, in being recorded with the USC Trojan Marching Band, set a record for the greatest number of musicians to appear on a chart single. In 1990, the females in the band, Stevie Nicks and Christine McVie, announced their departure from the line-up, leaving the door open for yet another set of variations on the Fleetwood Mac theme.

INSET: The original Fleetwood Mac line-up, with guitar guru Peter Green dressed in red robe.

BELOW: The Macs in their most successful incarnation, which produced the album *Rumours* that went on to sell 15 million copies.

GIGS

BELOW: The concert
held at Wembley
Stadium, London, to
celebrate Nelson
Mandela's 70th birthday
was an emotional and
uplifting occasion.

aul McCartney holds the record for the biggest attendance at a gig for a single billed artist. On his 1990 world-wide "Get Back" tour, Paul's date at the Maracana Stadium in Rio attracted an audience numbering an incredible 184,368, one of the largest paying crowds of fans ever assembled. The biggest gig that never happened was, of course, one of a selection of Beatles reunions tabled to occur throughout the seventies. The US promoter Bill Sargent offered the band a record $30 million to reunite for a single concert. The band declined, committing to legend a live act whose last performance was on the roof of their record company offices in Savile Row, London, in January 1969. The set was caught on celluloid and forms a major part of the end section of The Beatles' last film *Let It Be*, itself an Oscar winner for Best Film Music.

There are many potential claimants to the title of most star-studded gig, and the nature of rock 'n' roll performance is such that musical friends and associates often get up on stage to "jam". The event called "The Last Waltz" held on Thanksgiving Day, 1976, at The Winterland Stadium in San Francisco, California, was the official final performance of ex-Dylan cohorts The Band. Among the galaxy of stars participating in the tightly organized set of rock classics, caught on film by Martin Scorcese, were Eric Clapton, Ringo Starr, Muddy Waters, Ron Wood, Neil Young, Van Morrison, Joni Mitchell, Neil Diamond, and of course Bob Dylan. At the time, the concert and film represented the greatest concentration of contemporary American rock talent gathered together for a single performance as one musical entity.

Another gig worth a mention is Eric Clapton's rehabilitative concert at the Rainbow, London, in 1973, where Pete Townshend gathered together an all-star band as incentive to draw Clapton out of his heroin-induced shell. The group included Ron Wood from the Faces, Stevie Winwood and Jim Capaldi, and their rendition of Hendrix's "Little Wing" seemed eerily to summon up the ghost of Jimi himself.

For more information on spotting star-studded collective performances, check out the sections on Live Aid (see page 61), which also features information on benefits, and Woodstock (see page 116).

GUITAR HEROES

The guitar hero was a phenomenon born of the 1960s when blues-influenced guitarists such as Eric Clapton, Jeff Beck, and Jimmy Page created a hybrid style which melded heavily amplified electric guitar playing with the soulful character of the original blues giants of the forties and fifties. With a style directly traceable to the "Royal Family" of blues guitarists BB, Freddie and Albert King, the three would-be giants of the UK R 'n' B scene each followed a similar route to success on the world stage.

Clapton's stint with the Yardbirds brought him recognition as a guitar great, but feeling that the Yardbirds' sometimes lightweight pop style didn't offer the purity or room for expression he was seeking, he left to join John Mayall's Bluesbreakers. His place in the Yardbirds

was taken by Jeff Beck, whose time with the group produced four chart hits in 1966. Later that year he was joined on guitar by Jimmy Page and this is the line-up which can be spotted in Antonioni's trendy sixties murder mystery *Blow Up*.

Jeff Beck went on to carve a niche as one of the most sought-after session musicians in America and formed the super group Beck, Bogert and Appice, and Jimmy Page formed Led Zeppelin from the ashes of the Yardbirds, but it was Eric Clapton who assured himself of world-wide star status with an ever-changing career which encompassed Cream, Blind Faith, Derek and the Dominoes, The Plastic Ono Band and his present incarnation as a middle-of-the-road guitar hero complete with Armani suit.

BELOW: Albert King, whose style influenced the "guitar heroes" of the 1960s, was himself inspired by the guitar playing of T-Bone Walker. He plays a left-handed Gibson Flying Arrow guitar in an immediately recognizable style.

OPPOSITE: Eric Clapton established his reputation as a guitar virtuoso in the mid sixties, earning himself the nickname "God".

· GENESIS ·

Genesis have reached the status of superstar group in their long career which began in 1966, when Mike Rutherford, Tony Banks and Peter Gabriel found themselves in a band together at their exclusive private school in England's leafy Surrey.

Signed to Decca Records by a former pupil of the same school in the shape of Jonathan King, the band then embarked upon recording their first album, *From Genesis to Revelation*, during the school break in August 1968. When the LP was released in 1969, it sold less than 1,000 copies and did not bode well for the group's fortunes.

It was not until the awesomely talented Phil Collins joined in August 1970, and the management of the group of art-rockers was taken over by Tony Stratton-Smith, that the band's luck began to change. The addition of Steve Hackett on guitar the same year also helped to establish a distinctive sound. The seventies saw the band consolidate their position and move from strength to strength, although it was not until 1978 that they were to earn their first gold disc for the album *And Then There Were Three*.

The 1980s saw Genesis achieve the extraordinary feat of remaining intact as a chart act while simultaneously existing as a duo of major solo projects, in the shape of Mike and the Mechanics and Phil Collins – both of which acts continued to find favour in the charts on both sides of the Atlantic.

LEFT AND BELOW: Still beloved in the US and Europe for their unique brew of progressive jazz rock, British-style, Genesis band members have forged successful solo careers too.

HITS

The entire history of the music business is based upon that at once elusive but strangely copious commodity, "the hit". Whether a single or an album, the search for the hit has fuelled the desire for fame, money and acceptance which burns brightly in the breasts of executives and musicians alike.

The mechanism which determines just which records can be classified as hits revolves around the charts, an analytical system based mainly on unit sales, although in the US it is a combination of radio plays and sales which determines appearances in the Hot 100. The nature of a chart relying on sales or plays, or a combination of both, leaves the system open to abuse in the shape of hype (see page 43).

Notable hits include "Jailhouse Rock", the first to go straight in at number one in the singles charts, and "Hey Jude", the longest continuous single ever to have topped the charts, clocking in at an enormous seven minutes 10 seconds. Latterly, Bryan Adams has spent a record 14 weeks at the number-one slot in the UK, smashing the previous record of 11 weeks which had stood since the fifties.

Characteristically, McCartney also had a hand in another record-breaking hit, helping to pen and perform "Get Back", surprisingly the only Beatles single to make its chart debut at the number-one slot in the UK.

Although The Jackson Five hold a previously mentioned record of having achieved number-one status in the US charts with their first three singles, the feat has been equalled by other artists in the UK listings. Gerry and the Pacemakers rode the crest of the Merseybeat wave with a similar debut trio of smashes. In the eighties the outrageous Frankie Goes To Hollywood saw "Relax" (eerily featuring a B-side cover version of Gerry and The Pacemakers "Ferry 'Cross the Mersey"), "Two Tribes" and "The Power of Love" all go to the number-one slot. The first two singles gained the band record-breaking status on their own, making Frankie the only group to have their first two singles go platinum. The album from which these tracks were drawn, *Welcome to the Pleasure Dome*, holds the record for the UK's biggest album ship-out to date – in other words, the biggest number of units moved from warehouse to shops in one go.

In the late eighties the UK's Jive Bunny hopped up the charts to the number-one space with their first three records, thus equalling the feat. Jive Bunny continued to produce a number of equally bouncy recordings, but unfortunately their popularity began to wain as the UK public seemed to tire of their musical formula.

BELOW: **Gerry and the Pacemakers** – hitmakers *extraordinaire* – **sharing the secret of their success!**

Another fascinating and record-making hit fact concerns The Beatles, whose album track "With a Little Help from my Friends" became the only cover version to reach the number-one position in the UK singles chart on two separate occasions, performed by different artists. These were the gravel-voiced growler, the one and only Joe Cocker, and the Scottish band Wet Wet Wet.

The all-important biggest-selling UK single of all time (so far) is "Do They Know It's Christmas?" by the all-star conglomeration that went under the collective name Band Aid. The song went straight in at number one at Christmas 1984 and sold over three million copies. With a popular annual re-release topping up these sales, it is likely to hold this record for quite some time.

Libidinous LA layabouts, Bill Bailey's band Guns 'n' Roses, currently hold the much sought-after record that can only be achieved once in any given career, that of biggest-selling debut album, with a fittingly fantastic figures of 9 million sales world-wide.

BELOW: **Bryan Adams spent 14 weeks in the UK number one slot with "Everything I Do (I Do For You)". This smashed the previous record of 11 weeks held by Slim Whitman with "Rose Marie" in the summer of 1955.**

· HENDRIX ·

James Marshall Hendrix has the distinction of being the only rock legend with the marque of his guitar amplification as his middle name. Apart from this rather dubious honour, Hendrix redefined the parameters of what could be achieved with an electric guitar; Jimi was to his instrument what Miles and Bird, before him, were to theirs.

An artist of the stature of Hendrix would inevitably set the pace in terms of earnings, and true to form, Hendrix was the highest-paid performer at the Woodstock festival, receiving the princely sum of $125,000 for a few minutes of feedback-laden twanging which, nevertheless, sent the fans wild.

Jimi also enjoys the unique status of being the only rock 'n' roll telepath – his sensitivity to forthcoming events was highlighted on more than one occasion. In 1965, while recording in New York with soul superstar Curtis Knight, Jimi predicted his own death with uncanny accuracy when he informed Knight that he would be six feet under within five years. That night, he went on to record the eery song written by Knight titled "The Ballad of Jimi". On his final, abortive tour of Europe, Jimi left the stage in Denmark with the ominous words, "I've been dead a long time". Four days later, Hendrix was no longer with us.

It was only in death that Hendrix became a rock record-breaker, attaining the status of most prolific posthumous performer. While alive, a scant five albums made their way into the eager clutches of his fans, but subsequent to his death, over three hundred different releases have found their way into the record racks.

RIGHT: **By 1967, Hendrix had done a successful tour of Britain, Germany and Scandinavia and had record success with "Hey Joe" and "Purple Haze". His appearance at the Monterey Pop Festival made him a star.**

HYPE

ABOVE: **U2 pictured enjoying a playback of their single "The Fly".**

hose four lads from Liverpool who shook the world didn't invent hype, but they weren't above it either. The fact that manager Brian Epstein owned the company NEMS that just happened to be the biggest distributor of records in the Midlands and north of England in the early sixties didn't help the band's first single "Love Me Do" achieve a national top-20 placing. Or did it?

Arriving in a foreign country to find that the advance publicity is defining you as "the future of rock 'n' roll" may well damage self-confidence or even create something approaching incredulity in record buyers, but in the crazy world of rock 'n' roll, such things do happen.

Jon Landau, noted critic on top US rock rag *Rolling Stone*, witnessed two shows by the then up-and-coming, car-made crooner Bruce Springsteen in Cambridge, Massachusetts in May 1974. His subsequent review stated, "I saw rock and roll future – and its name is

Bruce Springsteen." Such ungrammatical hyperbole led the CBS press office to pounce upon the phrase and create a spurious, but none the less enviable profile for Springsteen as the saviour and the future of rock 'n' roll. Such was the currency and appeal of this idea, that the UK division of the company undertook an extensive poster campaign to pave the way for the man himself. When Springsteen arrived on British soil he was reputedly outraged at the hyped-up claims that were being made on his behalf. Or was he?

The success of any form of hype, which is essentially a method of inflating the consumer's desire for products which often appear to possess little or no intrinsic worth, relies on the cynical ability of the hyper and the gullibility of the reader. Rock music abounds with examples of record company practice bordering on the sharp in order to stimulate demand for the products of their protégés. Techniques for hyping range from the mundane, such as employing teams of people to buy the records from the shops, to the absurd. The late 1970s and early eighties saw a mania for coloured vinyl and picture discs create a situation where many records were released in anything up to 10 marginally different versions, in the hope that vinyl junkies on the streets would buy more than one copy of an identical recording simply because the format was slightly different. Because the UK charts are compiled using sales of all formats as one release, a slightly delayed release of a version containing extra tracks or remixes can often be used to extend the chart life of a record. The first and, some would argue, most assuredly handled release which used this technique of hype was Frankie Goes To Hollywood's first single "Relax", which initially appeared on 7-inch, 12-inch, cassette and picture disc, and then subsequently as seven different remixes. The record took 10 weeks to climb to the top slot of the UK singles chart and sold more than 1 million copies in the process.

More recently, the art of hyping took a different and inventive turn when U2 topped the UK singles chart in October 1991 with "The Fly". The unusual move of U2 releasing a single was compounded by the hyping technique employed by their record company, Island. In order to concentrate the sales over a relatively small

period of time and therefore ensure a high chart placing, it was made known that the record would be deleted from the catalogue after only three weeks on sale. So successful was the technique, Island are now rumoured to be considering employing the sales technique with all their releases.

ABOVE: **The Beastie Boys were marketed in the late eighties as pop music's new hell-raisers. Sadly, they proved too clean-cut and well-behaved to sustain the hype.**

HAIRCUT

Private Presley, E. US Army 53310761
"Rock and roll died the day Elvis joined the army."
– John Lennon.

RIGHT: **The King lost his crowning glory courtesy of a US Army barber.**

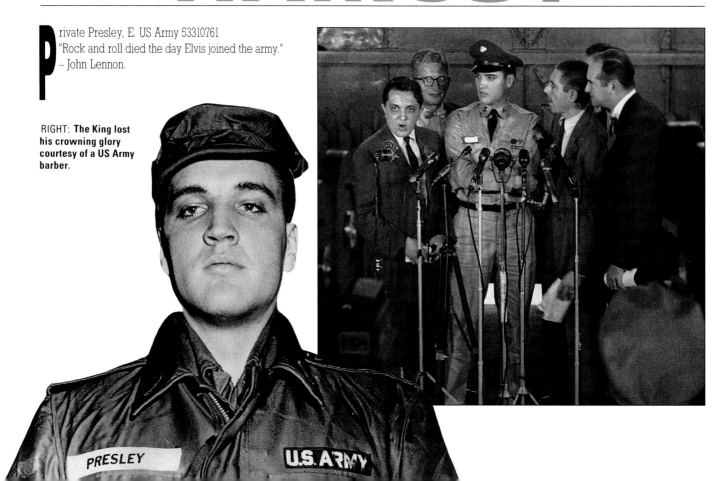

HI-TECH

In the 1980s many industries shed manpower, increased production and delegated work to unskilled labour. The music industry was no exception, and the key to the production of music by means other than real musical instruments lay in wide-scale automation. The first use of this phenomenon was for drumming. Linn Industries were the first to manufacture a usable drum machine in the Linndrum. Machines of this ilk enabled the DIY ethic of the late 1970s' punk explosion to be taken up by exponents of a burgeoning dance movement: Arthur Baker, Frankie Knuckles and Giorgio Moroder. Such is the prevalence of automated rhythm tracks that the Roland 808 drum machine has provided most of the kick and snare sounds on rap and dance tracks through the 1980s. If you wish to pursue this line of thought, turn to "Sampling" (page 100).

LEFT: Giorgio Moroder, pioneer of the automated drumbeat, left an indelible mark on the disco scene of the seventies in his work with Donna Summer, among others.

BELOW AND INSET: Paisley Park studios is the hi-tech artistic base for diminutive pop star Prince, in his home town of Minneapolis.

IMAGE

Success in the music business does not rely on simply how good an artist might sound; it also has a great deal to do with how the artist looks. As Shakespeare once said, "Clothes maketh the man". Therefore the role of the image maker in the music business has become pivotal in the process by which artists are groomed for public consumption.

Take, for example, the case of Paul Raven (né Gadd) who, by the late sixties, had spent several unsuccessful years slogging away in pursuit of the previously mentioned, elusive commodity, the hit record. By the early seventies, Raven had noticed the first stirrings of what was to become known as "glam rock". A man of restrained taste and good business sense, he first rejected the names Terry Tinsel and Stanley Sparkle before alighting on the altogether more appealing Gary Glitter. In this new guise he achieved record-breaking status by effecting the most astounding overnight change of image ever. Glitter (né Raven, né Gadd) carried out his next move, which was to assemble a similarly attired group of musicians, whom he imaginatively dubbed The Glitter Band. Their first single, the 15-minute double A-sided "Rock 'n' Roll Parts 1 and 2", went on to become a top 10 hit on both sides of the Atlantic, and there were many more UK and worldwide chart successes in the years to come.

INSET: **Paul Raven rejected the names Terry Tinsel and Stanley Sparkle before opting for the even more flashy Gary Glitter.**

LEFT: **Gary Glitter stood head and shoulders above his glam-rock-era peers (note footwear).**

IMPORTS

Some records do not gain immediate release on a world-wide basis, despite demand for the product. Often, in such cases, enterprising shops or individuals will take it upon themselves to order and ship the records from the territory in which they have been released in order to sell them at a premium price to the waiting fans.

The Clash's first album *The Clash* has already been mentioned. Another of the UK's top punk trio, The Jam, went on to become the record holders for the highest UK chart hit single available only on import, when the acoustically rendered "That's Entertainment" hit the top 20 in February 1981.

LEFT: **The Jam's Paul Weller strums "That's Entertainment", the highest import-only chart entry in the UK singles listings.**

BELOW: **100,000 copies of *The Clash*, the first album by the band of the same name, were shipped out to the US – making it a record.**

· INXS ·

ABOVE: **Michael Hutchence of INXS,** apparently unconcerned about inflaming the desires of the world's female population.

INXS, featuring the tightly betrousered sex-god Michael Hutchence, hold the record for the most appearances of a band by satellite, by the simple expedient of the fact that they live in Australia. Their "out of this world" career began with the group's participation in Live Aid in 1985 and most recently saw Hutchence and the band firing on all cylinders at the Simple Truth Kurdish Benefit in 1990. AC/DC, however, hold the record of being the first antipodean rockers to gain worldwide acceptance.

THIS PAGE: In the past five years, INXS has taken Europe and the US by storm, spearheading a renaissance in Aussie rock.

OPPOSITE: Michael Hutchence and INXS enjoy truly global success, along with other Australian rockers Midnight Oil and, before them, AC/DC.

JAIL

he rebel image cultivated by the early rockers saw many brushes with the law, but Chuck Berry, to some the "father of rock 'n' roll", appropriately enough became the first to "do some time". After being sentenced to five years imprisonment in 1959 on charges of violation of the Mann Act (which forbids the transportation of women from one state to another for immoral purposes), Berry was eventually incarcerated after a retrial in 1962. He served two years of a three-year term. The rocking recidivist returned to his cell in 1979 for five months on charges of income tax evasion. They say bad luck always comes in threes, and true to form, in 1989 police raided Berry's home and took away films, videos, firearms and exotic tobacco. Consequently he was subjected to a further six months in prison.

Berry-influenced rocker Keith Richards took his admiration for his mentor a little too far, not only borrowing Chuck's tunes, riffs, licks and general guitar style but also aspects of his lifestyle as well. In 1967 the arrest of Richards and Jagger at Keith's Surrey mansion, Redlands, caused a shockwave of indignation to run through the more enlightened elements of the establishment. The British idea of "fair play" was called into question, with William Rees Mogg's leader in *The Times* newspaper highlighting the fact that the harsh sentences meted out to the duo were akin to "breaking a butterfly on a wheel". The publicity generated by the trial, especially concerning the confectionary-consuming habits

of Marianne Faithfull Jagger's then girlfriend, helped confirm the Rolling Stones' status as the official "bad boys" of rock. It is doubtful whether such publicity could have been bought for less than the £14,000 Jagger and Richards ended up paying by way of a fine.

Some would say that to witness a Richards solo gig is a trial, but his sentencing by Judge Lloyd Graburn in Toronto in 1978 is a record in itself. After arrest by the Mounties, Richards escaped a lengthy prison term by agreeing to perform a concert for the Canadian National Institute for the Blind, after a personal appeal from a blind, though obviously not deaf fan. The event took place on 22 April 1979, when Richards assembled an all-star line-up including Ian Mclagan, Stanley Clark, Bobby Keyes and of course, fellow Stone Ron Wood, who himself was jailed the following year for possession of illegal substances.

Finally, mention has to be given to the Georgia jailbird himself, James Brown. In and out of jail more times than can be set out here, Brown's most recent visit to a state penitentiary was in 1988, when he was incarcerated for a term of six years on charges resulting from a spectacular car chase. Six months later Brown underlined his respect for the law and for the correctional facilities placed at his disposal, when he was moved to a more secure establishment after prison officers found over $40,000 in cheques and cash hidden in his cell.

BELOW: **After a childhood stint at reform school, Chuck Berry was jailed on two separate occasions for violating the Mann Act and income tax evasion.**

· JACKO ·

Few people in the world of entertainment, let alone the music industry, can claim to equal the achievements of Michael Jackson. In a career spanning almost a quarter of a century, Jackson has set, broken and made many records, not the least of which occurred when he was but 10 years old.

In 1969, the tuneful tot, as a member of Berry Gordy's protégé group The Jackson Five, had a number-one hit on both sides of the Atlantic with "I Want You Back", making him the youngest lead singer of a group to achieve such a feat. It seemed not to matter that the pint-sized, piccolo-voiced singer was putting his heart and soul into the delivery of a set of lyrics dealing with the adult subject of lost love – the public

took him to their hearts. Two years later, Jackson had his first solo success with the plaintive "Got To Be There", another strikingly adult song, sung in falsetto by the 13-year-old chanteur. There then followed a run of four years of hits on Motown Records before Michael and his brothers signed to Epic in 1975.

The first fruits of the new deal with Epic marked a change in musical direction with "Don't Stop Till You Get Enough", providing Jackson with his first US number one for seven years. The song also helped the album *Off the Wall* to sell over 10 million copies world-wide. By the time the ballad "She's Outta My Life" was lifted from the album to become a top-10 hit on both sides of the Atlantic, Jackson had become the first

solo artist to have four hit singles released from one album.

In 1982, Jackson wrote a song for his long-time friend Diana Ross called "Muscles". It was titled after his pet python, the first animal in Jacko's personal menagerie. Such was Jackson's growing fascination with animals that his zoo of constant companions was to expand over the next few years. The chimpanzee Bubbles caused some problems on his arrival in Britain to attend his friend and master's record

ABOVE: The self-proclaimed "King of Pop" pictured with some early members of his animal entourage.

LEFT: **Michael Jackson
had his first
transatlantic chart-
topper in 1969 at the
tender age of 10, along
with his brothers in the
Jackson 5 – "I Want You
Back".**

OPPOSITE: **Michael
Jackson on stage in
Tokyo in 1988.**

seven sell-out nights at London's
Wembley arena, as customs officials
could not allow the furry fan into the
country due to strict quarantine laws.

It was in 1983 that Jackson's record-
breaking status was to reach a highspot.
With the success of the single "Billie
Jean", the accompanying video was the
first by a black artist to achieve airplay
on MTV. In so doing, the track elevated
the fortunes of the parent album
Thriller, which went on to break all
previous records by becoming the most
successful album of all time, selling over
40 million world-wide and hitting the
number-one slot in every Western
country, including a record 37 weeks at
number one in the US album charts. The
album sold over 1 million copies in Los
Angeles alone, received a record 12
Grammy nominations and caused
Jackson to break his own record by
spawning seven US top-10 hit singles.

The record-breaking feats did not stop
there as the title track of the album,
featuring the voice of Vincent Price, is
the subject matter for the longest
promotional video ever. Directed by
John Landis, the full length *Thriller*
promo clocked in at over 20 minutes,
and won a Grammy for its trouble.
Furthermore, the film made about its
conception and production became the
biggest-selling music video ever.

Other Jackson records include being
the first non-Soviet citizen allowed to
advertise a produce on CCCP-TV and
being the only star to offer $50,000 for
the remains of John Merrick – the
Elephant Man. In a further display of
his acquisitive streak, Jackson also
outbid Paul McCartney and Yoko Ono
for the rights to the ATV music
publishing catalogue. For $47.5 million
Jacko became the proud owner of
thousands of songs, including 250
written by Lennon and McCartney.

In 1991, Michael announced the
signing of the most lucrative recording
contract ever, when Sony advanced the
singer a staggering $18 million in crisp,
US greenbacks.

KILLING

t could be argued that the whole of the music business is predicted on the idea of making a "killing". Some, however, have taken this notion a little further than necessary.

Widely acknowledged as the first rock 'n' roll fatality was the classically named Johnny Ace, whose death on Christmas Day in 1954 remains shrouded in mystery. Backstage at "The Negro Christmas Dance" at the City Auditorium in Houston Texas, Ace died of gunshot injuries. Some stories held that the fatal shots were fired by his own hand, others embellished this tale with stories of Russian roulette, and the more off-the-wall theories spoke of a hired contract killer carrying out the callous deed. Whatever the truth of the matter, Ace was assured of his place in the rich mythology of rock music.

RIGHT AND OPPOSITE: On 8 December 1980, John Lennon was murdered by Mark Chapman outside his apartment block in New York – a cruelly ironic end for one of rock's great peace campaigners.

BELOW: Terry Kath, guitarist with Chicago, died from a firearms accident at a friend's home.

Another tragic case is that of the soul genius Marvin Gaye, whose career had been revived in 1982 with a move from Motown to CBS Records and the release of "(Sexual) Healing", which sold over a million copies and was the first record to top the US R 'n' B charts for 10 weeks since 1962. After moving to live with his parents in Los Angeles, Gaye attempted to take his own life on more than one occasion. In what must rank as one of the most bizarre killings of a star of Marvin Gaye's status, he departed this world at the hands of the man who helped bring him into it: Gaye Snr shot his son dead on 1 April 1984 – yet another needless rock tragedy.

Other rockers have found that their fascination with firearms can lead to a premature departure. Chicago's founder and lead guitarist, Terry Kath, sadly met his end while checking out the gun collection of a friend. Juggling with what he believed to be an unloaded weapon, the gun went off, killing Kath, but this tragedy failed to halt Chicago in their inexorable and long-lived success story.

A gruesome record goes to the members of Apple signings and McCartney protégés Badfinger, whose principle songwriters Pete Ham and Tom Evans, together responsible for the world-wide multimillion-selling song "Without You", died in identical circumstances, committing suicide by the expedient of hanging themselves in a garage, albeit eight years apart.

John Lennon was shot dead at 10.50pm in New York on 8 December 1980, snuffing out any hope of a Beatles reunion, in this world at least.

· B.B. KING ·

Born in 1925, it could be assumed that the King of the Blues is way too old for inclusion in a text devoted to the music of the young, but his place in the annals of rock record-breaking is both assured and deserved.

By 1955, King was in the middle of a five-year run of US R 'n' B chart success. At that time, with the race laws in full operation, it was impossible for a black artist to cross over into the white-oriented mainstream charts. King was averaging over 300 gigs a year, a schedule he maintained well into the 1970s. By the end of the 1960s, however, King's legendary status had been fully established by the open acknowledgement of his influence from a new generation of rock stars in the shape of Beck, Clapton and Page. His new-found, and widely accepted, status as one of the elder statesmen of the electric guitar, led to live appearances at rock-based festivals alongside artists such as Jimi Hendrix, Creedence Clearwater Revival, The Byrds, Jefferson Airplane, Janis Joplin and Led Zeppelin. It was at this point in his long and awe-inspiring career that King crossed over into mainstream chart success and acknowledgement by an indebted musical establishment. King won his first Grammy in 1982, followed by two more in 1984 and 1986. There then followed induction into rock 'n' roll's prestigious Hall of Fame at its second annual dinner in 1987.

In 1988, King was honoured at the 30th annual Grammy awards with a lifetime achievement award. The summary of his career included the following praise: "King is one of the most original and soulful of all blues guitarists and singers, whose compelling style and devotion to the musical truth have inspired so many budding performers, both here and abroad, to celebrate the blues."

In 1990, the accolades continued to mount up with the Lifetime Achievement Awards at the Songwriters Hall of Fame 21st Induction. That year he also left his prints in the celestial cement of the Hollywood Walk of Fame and by 1991, King was so feted that the Gibson guitar company honoured him with yet another Lifetime Achievement Award at New York's Hard Rock Café for spending more than 30 years running his subtly supple fingers over the body and neck of "Lucille" – his trusty geetar.

OPPOSITE: An early shot of B.B. King, flanked by Evelyn Young and Bill Harvey.

LEFT: U2 sought the help of B.B. King for "Love Comes to Town" and on their *Rattle and Hum* tour.

KINGS

The royalty of rock 'n' roll reside in regal splendour in the memories of rock fans throughout the world. The hit-makers' hierarchy consists of a lineage which is traceable back through more than 40 years of music making.

From the blues and R 'n' B roots, out of which the great family tree of rock 'n' roll grew, came the magical magi of rock's very own royal family. At the top of the tree were the three Kings: B.B., Albert and Freddie. Although unrelated by blood, their bond was that forged by a mastery of the blues guitar. Their influence clearly can be found in the work of their princely protégés, Clapton, Beck and Page, whose guitar pyrotechnics in the sixties brought the music of their majestic mentors to a wider rock audience.

Other notable kings include Carole King, who after writing dozens of hits throughout the sixties in partnership with Gerry Goffin, then went on to release her own album *Tapestry* in 1970 which sold 15 million copies

ABOVE: Blues monarch Freddie King first jammed with Muddy Waters in Chicago. Over a six year peiod, Federal released 77 titles by King via singles and albums, 30 of which were instrumentals.

LEFT: Carole King's album *Tapestry* sold 15 million copies in 1970.

world-wide, a record for a solo female artist. Mention must be made of The Kingsmen, whose recording of "Louie Louie" in 1963 sold over a million and introduced to the world a rock standard whose influence on the use of the three-chord trick has been subsequently immeasurable.

In spite of these pretenders to the throne, there was and is only one true King of Rock 'n' Roll. His Camelot was Gracelands, his Excalibur a guitar, his subjects included every music fan in the world. His name will live on forever more.

LIVE AID

The power and emotion elicited by the very best of rock music as been, on occasion, harnessed to produce an expression of our fragile Earth as a true "Global Village".

In 1967 the first worldwide "live" television link-up was broadcast to over 400 million people, with The Beatles singing "All You Need Is Love" as its highlight. A panoply of popsters gathered in the famous Abbey Road studios, including Jagger and Richards, Clapton, The Walker Brothers, Graham Nash and Keith Moon for the ground-breaking broadcast, which was arranged to raise awareness of poverty in the Third World.

The next event to provide evidence of rock's growing global conscience was the massive benefit staged at Madison Square Garden over two days in August 1971. Masterminded by George Harrison at the suggestion of his friend Ravi Shankar, the Concert For Bangladesh saw the ex-Beatle joined by Bob Dylan, Eric Clapton, Ringo Starr, Leon Russell, Badfinger and Eastern superstar Ravi himself, whose 10-minute tuning-up drew applause from Westerners unused to the unusual tonal scales employed by Shankar and his coterie of skilled Eastern musicians.

It was not until 1985 that the potential of One World and of The Concert For Bangladesh was realized in the staging of the most important live event of the rock era. After witnessing a particularly harrowing account of the Ethiopian famine of 1984 broadcast by the BBC, Bob Geldof enlisted the help of friend Midge Ure to write the song "Do They Know It's Christmas?". On its release, the record, which featured a galactic line-up of superstars, became the biggest-selling UK single ever, with a five-week run at the top of the chart and sales in excess of 3 million.

This unprecedented success spawned a transatlantic response in the shape of "We Are The World", written by Lionel Richie and Michael Jackson, and recorded by a superstar collective known as USA For Africa. The single made number one all over the globe.

The enormous interest aroused by these records induced Geldof to consider staging a world-wide consciousness- and fund-raising event. At 12.01 British

LIVE AID

MAIN PHOTOGRAPH:
The momentous event that was Live Aid took place on 13 July 1985.

BELOW: **Bob Geldof and Chrissie Hynde of the Pretenders with fund-raising publication at the Hard Rock Café in New York.**

Summer Time, venerable boogie-merchants Status Quo had the honour of blasting out the first notes of John Foggerty's apposite anthem "Rocking' All Over The World". Live Aid had begun. Fuelled by credit-card donations and telephone pledges from the watching world, and administered with the help of major banks and international financial institutions, the money-making musical marathon was staged at two separate venues, with only the Atlantic Ocean between them.

In Wembley Stadium, London, and the massive JFK Stadium, Philadelphia, the list of participating per-

formers was simply staggering: Geldof himself, Paul Weller and the Style Council, Adam Ant, Midge Ure with Ultravox, Elvis Costello, Sade, Queen, Tears for Fears, Simple Minds, Hall and Oates, the Rolling Stones, The Who, Sting, Lionel Richie, David Bowie, the Pretenders, Tom Petty, The Cars, Neil Young, Paul McCartney, George Michael, Madonna, U2, Duran Duran, Bryan Adams, INXS, BB King, Brian Ferry, Paul Young, The Beach Boys, Dire Straits, Santana, Elton John, Powerstation, Bob Dylan, and an especially re-formed Led Zeppelin.

Phil Collins should be singled out for particular praise. As well as performing his own songs and playing drums with many artists, his transatlantic dash aboard the supersonic aircraft Concorde set a hitherto unimaginable record when he appeared on stage in two continents on the same day.

The final statistics speak for themselves. The event was witnessed by an estimated 2,000 million people across the world, with telethons and associated campaigns in 22 countries raising over $70 million.

Such was the enormous success of the venture that many subsequent fund-raising events took their lead from Live Aid, both in terms of the collection methods employed and the participatory nature of these charitable spectacles. Run the World saw yet another global television link-up using the ever-improving satellite technology which had made Live Aid possible. Although this was not a musical event, the global consciousness and the sense of responsibility generated by Live Aid was directly responsible for the event taking place. In charitable terms, Live Aid inspired many clones in the shape of Comic Relief in the UK and Farm Aid in the US.

BELOW: **Mark Knopfler of Dire Straits.**

BOTTOM: **George Michael.**

· LED ZEPPELIN ·

"The Nobs" was a pseudonym used by the band after a relative of Count Von Zeppelin, airship designer and friend of the Kaiser, threatened to sue them for unauthorised use of the name for a gig in Denmark, but, legal wrangles notwith-standing, the gig was played. The band took their real name from a favourite expression of Who drummer "Keith" Moon. He used the phrase to describe the audience reception to less than successful musical performances (i.e. "It went down like a . . .").

But by 1969, their second album had scotched any idea of dodgy musical competence with chart stays of 138 weeks in the UK and 98 weeks in the US. It was also a number one on both sides of the Atlantic. The following year the group was voted Top Group in the

Melody Maker Polls usurping The Beatles after eight years as readers' favourites. With the Fabs split and the Rolling Stones in inactive tax exile, Led Zep became the undisputed top group world-wide. They were the first group of global status to stipulate a clause in their recording contract that no singles should be released in the UK. For this reason, Zep were the first to introduce the concept of an "albums band".

In 1973, Zep broke the US attendance and box-office records with their show at Tampa Stadium, Florida. The Beatles had been the previous holders with their 1965 Shea Stadium gig.

Led Zeppelin are also responsible for the song "Stairway to Heaven" one of the longest and most requested radio plays throughout the world.

OPPOSITE : **Jimmy Page formed Led Zeppelin in 1968 out of the ashes of the Yardbirds.**

ABOVE: **Led Zeppelin became the biggest group in the world in the early seventies,** beating the Beatles' Shea Stadium show for attendance and box office receipts at Tampa Stadium in 1973.

MAKE-UP

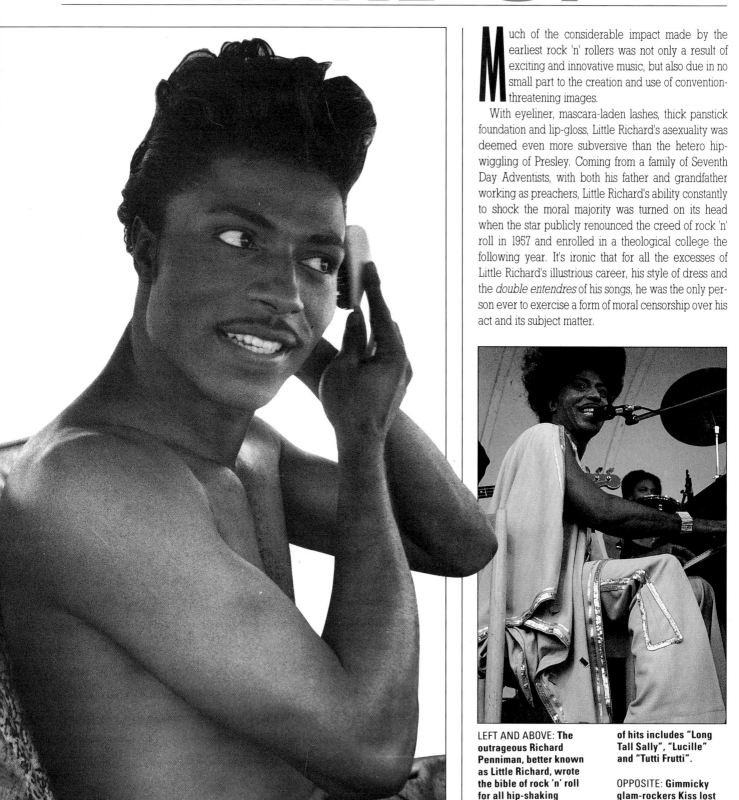

Much of the considerable impact made by the earliest rock 'n' rollers was not only a result of exciting and innovative music, but also due in no small part to the creation and use of convention-threatening images.

With eyeliner, mascara-laden lashes, thick panstick foundation and lip-gloss, Little Richard's asexuality was deemed even more subversive than the hetero hip-wiggling of Presley. Coming from a family of Seventh Day Adventists, with both his father and grandfather working as preachers, Little Richard's ability constantly to shock the moral majority was turned on its head when the star publicly renounced the creed of rock 'n' roll in 1957 and enrolled in a theological college the following year. It's ironic that for all the excesses of Little Richard's illustrious career, his style of dress and the *double entendres* of his songs, he was the only person ever to exercise a form of moral censorship over his act and its subject matter.

LEFT AND ABOVE: The outrageous Richard Penniman, better known as Little Richard, wrote the bible of rock 'n' roll for all hip-shaking screamers that ever tried to get an audience on its feet. His roll-call of hits includes "Long Tall Sally", "Lucille" and "Tutti Frutti".

OPPOSITE: Gimmicky glam-rockers Kiss lost their audience when they wiped off their make-up.

ABOVE: **The seminal
New York Dolls crossed
many image genres with
sensational style and
powerful shock value.**

The continuing ability of even the crudest forms of make-up to shock and outrage the establishment was next drawn upon by the Rolling Stones in October 1966, when they were photographed on New York's Park Avenue in full drag to publicize the single "Have You Seen Your Mother Baby Standing in the Shadows", thereby claiming a record as the first band to employ cross-dressing as a promotional gimmick. Later, in 1974, Jagger denied the imminent recruitment of guitarist

Ron Wood with the telling quote: "No doubt we can find a brilliant six foot three blonde guitarist who can do his own make-up".

American heavy-rockers Kiss took the whole thing a stage further, refusing to be interviewed unless they were wearing their full stage make-up of white foundation and black detailing. The band traded on the gimmick image for nine years but in August 1983, a three-day tour of Argentina was cancelled at the last

moment after the Free Fatherland Nationalist Commando Movement threatened to stop the tour even if they had to "go so far as to cost the very lives of that unfortunate band". Coincidentally, the band made their first public appearance without their shocking make-up on MTV the following month. No one recognized them.

Although the New York Dolls heralded yet another British dalliance with make-up in the shape of punk, it was George O'Dowd, better known as Boy George, who capitalized upon the excesses of the short-lived New Romantic movement in the early eighties. Thanks solely to his extraordinary appearance, he had made himself a magnet for photographers and gossip columnists on the late-seventies London club scene. In inventing a look which amalgamated the glamour of thirties and forties film stars with a range of multi-cultural "visual quotes", Boy George, with Culture Club, found global acceptance for the latest variation on the use of face paint.

ABOVE AND TOP: **Boy George** caused widespread confusion with his "gender bender" image and his admission that he preferred a nice cup of tea to sex!

MERCHANDISING

The music industry not only generates money through the sales of records, tapes and more recently CDs, but also through the assorted connected paraphernalia and ephemera that constitutes the merchandising associated with successful acts.

This area, often blurring the boundaries between authorized "official" items and the wide-ranging products of the pirating entrepreneurs, is responsible for the generation of vast amounts of revenue. Although Elvis Presley was marketed with considerable aplomb by his manager "Colonel" Tom Parker, it was The Beatles who were the first artistes to enjoy the full exploitation of the merchandisers.

Some months before the first visit to America by the group, their manager Brian Epstein signed a deal on their behalf authorizing the use of their name, likeness and image in associated products. The result was that the American public, already buying Beatles records in their millions, were to be offered a wide range of items endorsed by and featuring their new-found objects of affection. Over two million T-shirts were bought prior to the band's arrival on US soil, and plastic guitars, badges, dolls and bubble gum were all sold in connection with the Liverpool lads. At Capitol Records, The Beatles' American label, even the top executives of the company were featured in promotional photographs wearing the ubiquitous, plastic Beatle-wigs.

Perhaps the most explicit example of excessive entrepreneurial enthusiasm was when, in 1965, some pillowcases which had cosseted those four famous mop-topped heads were taken from a hotel, sliced into 160,000 pieces and sold to frantic fans for the premium price of a dollar each.

Although The Beatles set the pattern for successive marketing campaigns, to the extent of being the subjects of the first rock-inspired television cartoon series, the group broke up before being able to exploit their sales potential to the extremes later realized by the likes of fellow sixties superstars the Rolling Stones. Jagger and Co's world-wide trip under the banner of the Steel Wheels tour in 1989 broke merchandising records all over the globe, with the most popular items being their extensive lines of designer clothing featuring the famous lips 'n' tongue logo.

ABOVE: **MC Hammer's plastic pals look just like the real thing.**

OPPOSITE, ABOVE: **The Who were cleverly manipulated by a succession of crafty managers wishing to** capitalize on the mod cult then sweeping London. Mod merchandise from 1964.

OPPOSITE, BELOW: **The Beatles were the first group to be fully exploited by the various** merchandising industries – in this case, in the form of cigarette cards.

MOVIES

"Rock Around The Clock" was released in 1956 to capitalize upon the emergent rock 'n' roll phenomenon, and was the first, fully fledged rock 'n' roll movie ever. Featuring a chubby Bill Haley, already in his thirties and with five kids at home, it caused riots in cinemas in the UK, where a dearth of live exposure to the nascent musical style left a frustrated audience ready to vent their pent-up passions on cinema seating.

The wily "Colonel" Tom Parker had already negotiated his client Elvis Presley's entry into the hallowed portals of Hollywood, resulting in his debut feature "Love Me Tender". Such was Presley's popularity at this early point in his career that the film was rewritten and re-shot to include four musical numbers. Twentieth Century-Fox released a record 550 prints of the film to American theatres, and furthermore, the film recouped its million dollar budget within the first week. The title track from the film also went on to become the first single ever to achieve advance orders of a million copies. Elvis' film career continued with contracted movies for the producer Hal Wallis but the next record to be established by the young singer was with *Jailhouse Rock*. The title song of this Presley vehicle became the first record ever to enter the UK charts at number one, selling over 500,000 copies in its first three days in the record shops.

The "rockumentary", which attempts to capture the essence of life on the road, was successfully parodied by Rob Reiner's 1984 feature *This Is . . . Spinal Tap*, but the first serious attempt to produce a rock feature relying on verité techniques and a mixture of concert footage and apparently unrehearsed and candid backstage footage, was D.A. Pennebaker's fly-on-the-wall version of life on the road with the young Bob Dylan, *Don't Look Back*. Released in 1965 to critical acclaim, the film revealed the pressures under which Dylan was operating as his fame grew in Britain where the tour was filmed. It's interesting to note the similarities in structure and content between Pennebaker's ground-breaking effort and the more recent (1991) movie by Alex Kershishian, *Truth or Dare – In Bed With Madonna,* which also used a mixture of backstage, hotel and live footage to create a believable, realistic and telling documentary movie. Pennebaker, apparently unwittingly, created a genre.

An innovative film which set the tone for many subsequent movie releases of the seventies was the documentary resulting from the three-day Woodstock Festival. Utilizing split-screen techniques, Mike Wadleigh's Oscar-winning 1970 movie *Woodstock* did its best to capture the atmosphere in the audience and the

ABOVE: **A promotional picture released just prior to the mischievous documentary *Truth or Dare – in Bed with Madonna.***

TOP: *Rock Around the Clock* **was the first ever fully fledged rock 'n' roll movie.**

RIGHT: **Most would agree that *Jailhouse Rock* (1957) is Elvis's best movie; indeed his four pre-Army films are in a different class from the later insipid money-spinners.**

aspirations of the bands participating in the last great hippie round-up on Max Yasgur's farm in New York State, in 1969. The movie received the Oscar for Best Feature-Length Documentary, and remains a powerful and evocative documentary of the last great happening of the age of peace and love.

· MADONNA ·

MADONNA
BLOND AMBITION
WORLD TOUR 90

4/20金,21土,22日 阪急西宮球場
■主催:読売テレビ 日本テレビ放送網マドンナコンサート委員会
■協賛:エルセーヌ,ニチレイ,日清サラダ油 ,ネスカフェ
■後援:FM大阪 Sony(エニィ)
■協力:ワーナー・パイオニア・特別協力:日本生命
■招待:富山化学セゾングループ
■製作:キョード・東京キョード一大阪

In 1985, Madonna consolidated her position on the UK music scene with her smash dance hit "Into The Groove" on the back of the hit film *Desperately Seeking Susan*. This was followed up with the re-release of "Holiday" which swiftly manouevred itself into the number-two slot, making Madonna the only female artist to occupy the top two spaces simultaneously, with only The Beatles, John Lennon and Frankie Goes To Hollywood having managed to achieve a similar feat.

Later that year, with the success of "Dress You Up" marking Madonna's eighth UK top-10 hit of 1985 (eight hits in one year constituting a record in itself), she became the only woman in 30 years to have three records jostling for position in the UK top 15.

In 1986, the album *True Blue* topped the charts in 28 different countries, a feat never before achieved by any other

artist, male or female. In 1987, with "La Isla Bonita", Madonna became the only female artist to have notched up four UK number ones.

In 1989 Madonna signed an enormous endorsement deal with Pepsi Cola and became the first artist to use a song in a promotional campaign before its official retail release – a smart move by anyone's standards. The same year "Express Yourself" hit number two in the US singles charts and saw Madonna overtake The Beatles on the list of all-time consecutive top five hits with a total of 16.

As good as this figure is, she is still some way behind the King, whose total is a mind-boggling 24.

The records kept falling to the ruby-lipped chanteuse when "Rescue Me" entered the US singles chart at Number 15 in 1991, making it the highest entry by a female artist ever.

Madonna, in a video still of the classic modern hit "Material Girl", openly indulging in her Monroe wannabee phase (opposite). La Ciccone's 1990 Blonde Ambition tour broke box office records around the world (top). At an Aids Benefit dancethon in LA (above).

NOISE

LEFT: **The pill-popping rebelliousness of the Who found its full expression in the excitement and sheer noise of the group's live performance.**

RIGHT: **Loud and dangerous – particularly for pigeons! – wildman of rock, Ted Nugent.**

BELOW: **With the possible exception of Jimi Hendrix, sullen Scottish boys Jesus and Mary Chain are the only group to have based a whole career on feedback.**

Since the dawn of rock 'n' roll, parents exposed to its perceived subversive sounds have denounced the resulting racket as nothing more than noise.

The first record actually to feature "noise" was "Anyway, Anyhow, Anywhere" by The Who. Described by writer Pete Townshend as "anti-middle aged, anti-boss class, and anti-young marrieds", the record's use of howling feedback caused US label Decca to return the masters to producer Shel Talmy thinking that the tapes had an inherent fault. The record went on to become a UK top-10 hit, and the popular UK television show "Ready Steady Go" (the forerunner of "Top of the Pops") adopted the track as its theme tune.

With the advances in amplification technology in the later sixties, volume became an integral element of the emergent Heavy Metal and Progressive Rock scenes. Led Zeppelin were renowned for their use of loudness as a musical tool, but it was US wildman rocker Ted Nugent whose onstage decibel level was so extreme that his is the only act on record as having disintegrated a pigeon innocently passing his PA stacks.

The only group to base a whole career on the use of feedback noise is the Jesus and Mary Chain. The Scottish brothers Jim and William Reid gained notoriety with their early singles "Upside-Down" and "Never Understand", which featured classic pop melodies swathed in a swirling soundscape of sonic squeals, making them the first group to gain a major record deal and a legion of fans by deliberately messing up the production of their own records.

· NEW ORDER ·

The members of Manchester's New Order, who rose phoenix-like from the ashes of Joy Division in 1980, hold the record for having chosen two of the most contentious names for their band, a reputation gained via accusations of Nazi connotations at the hands of certain irresponsible sections of the tabloid press.

New Order were also the first British post-punk band to make any significant inroads into the US dance market. Their 1983 collaboration with Arthur Baker saw the release of "Blue Monday", which when it hit the streets in April of that year reached number 12 in the singles charts. It remained in the top 100 until October, when it climbed back up the charts to become a top-10 hit. Eventually, "Blue Monday" went on to become the biggest-selling 12"-single, with world-wide sales of over 3 million.

New Order have built much of their reputation and their musical style on a ready acquaintance with the latest in musical technology. In 1987, the singles collection *Substance* saw the first European commercial release of an album by a chart act on Digital Audio Tape. A rash move, some would say, as the number of domestically owned DAT machines had barely crept into double figures. Nevertheless, a first is a first.

By 1989, their status was such that their sixth album *Technique* entered the UK album chart at number one. As a footnote, the same year saw singer/guitarist Bernard Sumner form his own supergroup with ex-Smiths axeman Johnny Marr and the Pet Shop Boys.

RIGHT: **New Order's** "Blue Monday" is the world's best-selling 12-inch-only single.

OFFSPRING

"Rock 'n' roll" is a euphemism for the sexual act, and the result of "reelin' and a-rockin'", "flip, flopping and flying" or "shaking, rattling and rolling" by rock stars themselves has often led to the extension of their dynastic lines in the shape of various curiously named offspring. And The Beatles were served a record-breaking string of hopeful, but doomed, paternity suits during their early tours around the globe.

In 1969, Frank Zappa (his real name) started a trend which was to bring smiles to the faces of pastors and Registrars of Births alike the world over. That year, Zappa married his second wife, Gail, and between them they were to produce two sons and two daughters. These children were given a head-start in life when they were imaginatively named Dweezil, Ahmet Rodan, Moon Unit and Diva, thereby assuring Zappa his place in the history of rock as the most bizarre and innovative namer of his children.

David Bowie also dabbled in dubious dubbing, calling his young son Zowie. The name may have been something of a publicity stunt or simply an extension of the Thin White Duke's boisterous bonhomie. Whatever the case, it was fortunate that Bowie did not insist on his son changing his name every time Dad changed his image. Perhaps significantly, young Zowie now prefers to be known by the more normal nomenclature of Joe.

Pop stars' predelictions for strange names for their children reached extremes when the Geldofs, St. Bob and his lovely wife Paula Yates, named their first daughter Fifi-Trixiebelle and her subsequent siblings Peaches and Pixie, so challenging Zappa on the grounds of inventiveness (as well as poor taste).

Julian Lennon with half-brother Sean and Yoko Ono (above). With mother Cynthia (below).

OPPOSITE: **Nancy Sinatra, whose boots were made for walkin' (or should it be "ridin'"?) lived in the shadow of her famous father and pop singer/ actor husband Tommy Sands until she teamed up with Lee Hazelwood in 1966. It was he that wrote the witty and aggressive "Boots".**

Frank Sinatra, who once castigated rock 'n' roll as "phoney and false, and sung, written, and played for the most part by cretinous goons" does not have his opinions on record concerning his daughter Nancy's appearance in the mid-sixties charts with the proto-feminist anthem "These Boots Are Made For Walking". The song heralded a long and fruitful collaboration by Nancy with Lee Hazelwood, the songwriter-producer behind many of the sounds and techniques which were to define the very parameters of rock 'n' roll.

For some unknown reason, having a father in a world-famous band is no guarantee of success. Take, for example, the case of the inventively named Zak Starkey, lesser-known son of better-known father, Ringo Starr. After spending a number of years pursuing an unsuccessful solo career, his highpoint was to appear with Ringo on the anti-apartheid waxing "Sun City" in 1985. He did provide his father with his very own record-breaking status as the first of The Beatles to become a grandfather, thereby causing a whole generation to feel that little bit older.

Julian Lennon, son of the famous John, deserves a mention in these pages for his decision to carry the Lennon musical dynasty forward with a series of strikingly original hits. The first of these, "Too Late For Goodbyes", was in 1984 and pinpointed the essence of Julian's style: a penchant for the plaintive mixed in with a healthy dose of short reverb on the vocals to make the most of vocal cords which are undeniably Lennon.

The path to pop stardom is a perilous one, particularly for the performing progeny of famous parents, who find themselves inevitably compared to their mothers and fathers, and so run the risk of charges of nepotism. The only way to prevent such charges sticking is to produce music of originality, quality and distinction.

· THE BIG "O" ·

oy Kelton Orbison had his first hit as a stablemate of the King at Sun Records. Released in 1956, Sun Catalogue Number 242 was "Ooby Dooby", which sold 350,000 copies and reputedly resulted in Orbison's nickname. It wasn't until 1960 that Orbison got his big breakthrough with "Only the Lonely", originally written with Elvis Presley in mind and later rejected by the Everley Brothers. It topped the UK singles charts and hit number two when recorded by the man who penned the song, The Big "O" himself. "Blue Angel", "I'm Hurtin'" and "Dream Baby" went on to make up a quartet of million-selling singles over the following two years.

Never one to underestimate the importance of a memorable image, Orbison holds the record for being the first artist to use shades, or dark glasses, as a trademark after an oversight caused him to leave his normal specs at home on the eve of his British tour with The Beatles. Unable to see without the aid of corrective eyewear, Roy was forced to keep wearing the dark ones, and by the end of his British sojourn, he found he was lumbered with a new, and extremely effective, image.

Although his career went from strength to strength, Orbison's personal life was not short on personal tragedy. After divorce from his wife Claudette in 1964, after her affair with their builder, the imaginatively named Braxton Dixon, Orbison married his childhood sweetheart the following year. But in 1966, tragedy struck when the Orbisons, each on their own heavily personalized motorcycle, were returning from the National Drag Racing meeting in Tennesse. A truck pulled out from a side-road near the town of Gallatin and killed Claudette.

A distraught Orbison threw himself into the care of his children. Unfortunately, fate was again unkind to

the leather-clad rocker. In September 1968, while Orbison was on tour in the UK, his home in Nashville was burnt to the ground and two of his beloved sons, Roy Jnr and Tony, were lost in the flames. The unluckiest man in rock? Decide yourself.

Before his own death in 1988, Orbison's career had seen a resurgence due to his involvement with the star-studded Traveling Wilburys. The Big "O" summed up the secrets of his own success more succinctly than any other, when he said, "Pack as much Poetry and Philosophy into a two-minute pop record as you can."

OPPOSITE: Orbison's rigid stage persona, complete with dark glasses, black outfit and, occasionally, motorcycle leathers, hid a man who was in fact painfully shy.

BELOW: The "Big O" had his first hit with Sun Records, legendary label and first home of Elvis Presley. It was "Ooby Dooby", first cut in 1956 with Orbison's own money.

PRODUCERS

Every industry has its behind-the-scenes heroes and back-room innovators; those people whose job it is to bring together technology and talent in the creation of desirable and commercially viable products. The music industry is no exception.

The early history of the record saw its function determined by its status as nothing more than a means of capturing live musical performance. The significant sojourns made by the Lomax brothers around the cotton fields of the southern states of the US in the thirties saw an excellent example of this. When their primitive direct-to-disc cuts captured the performance and essence of a whole host of blues legends, songs which otherwise would have been lost to subsequent generations were preserved. The Lomax brothers' record-breaking recordings now reside in the American Library of Congress.

As well as having a major impact on the development of rock 'n' roll with his pioneering work on the electric guitar, Les Paul was also at the forefront of the emergent studio recording technology. Paul was among the first to dabble with the innovative use of dubbing, and indeed holds the record for having the first multi-tracked recording commercially released, with his duet with wife Mary Ford on the song "How High The Moon?" in 1951. The use of this technique, which involves being able to record sounds over already-taped tracks without significant loss of quality, together with leaps in other areas of studio technology, led to the creation of a clearly defined role for "the producer".

By the mid-fifties Norman Petty was making a name for himself with his own studio in Clovis, New Mexico, and the work he did at the time with Buddy Holly and the Crickets helped further to define the role of the producer. Whereas Sam Phillips had a distinctive sound at his own Sun studios in Memphis, with its trademark reverb and reputation for rocking-up bluegrass- and country-influenced singers, Petty began to extend the role of producer into areas of arrangement, songwriting and recording techniques. The first fruits of the collaboration between Petty and Holly was the world-wide hit "That'll Be The Day", released in May 1957, and it became a blueprint for the pop single as an entity in its own right.

The man who made the role of producer into something more than an interpreter of other people's songs was the legendary Phil Spector. Spector was the first to have his own distinctive soundscape, a swathe of swirling reverbs that came together to form his unique, and much imitated, "wall of sound". Spector not only dictated the actual sound of his art, but wrote some top tunes too. His first major hit was "To Know HIm Is To Love Him" by the Teddybears in 1958. Spector's increasing use of studio time in his unquenchable quest for the perfect sound led to his recording of Gene Pitney's "Every Breath I Take" being the most expensive recording session of 1961, costing an enormous $14,000.

OPPOSITE: **George Martin (second from left) was at the forefront of studio advances in his work with the Beatles throughout the sixties.**

The sensitive and egocentric Phil Spector brought the art of record production to a new level of sophistication and complexity, and became the first producer to be more famous than his artists.

to salvage The Beatles' last commercial release *Let It Be*. The album is the only Beatles' LP released during the band's existence which did not feature George Martin in the producer's chair. Spector later went on to find further success working with ex-Beatles Harrison and Lennon on their solo projects, including Lennon's atmospheric "Imagine".

George Martin's work with The Beatles from their earliest sessions for the Parlophone label saw the first truly symbiotic relationship emerge between band and producer to the extent that, for many, Martin was "the fifth Beatle". Martin's classical background and his previous work recording orchestras as an EMI in-house producer led The Beatles to become the first rock band to experiment with a wide range of instrumentation. Their use of harpsichord on "In My Life", the string quartet on "Yesterday" and the tumultuous coda to "A Day In The Life" owe their existence in part to George Martin's influence and studio skills.

From the mid-eighties onward, the British singles charts were dominated by a talented trio known as SAW. Pete Waterman, a self-acknowledged salesman started his own PWL record label in the early eighties. Joining forces with studio wizards Mike Stock and Matt Aitken, both of whom came from solid backgrounds of session and production work, the three colleagues capitalized on the mania for dance-oriented pop by writing and producing early hits for Hazel Dean and Mel and Kim. SAW's subsequent career took them into the record books in no uncertain terms when they spent nearly a decade during which, at any time, a SAW record could be found in the top 40.

In the early sixties, Spector found his niche working with the female groups who were to make his name synonymous with a certain sound. The likes of The Ronettes, the Crystals, Darlene Love and others found that their records were increasingly referred to as "Phil Spector Records" – the producer-as-star had arrived.

Spector's status as a mystical musical guru continued throughout the sixties and appropriately, he resurfaced

Born Prince Nelson Rogers in Minneapolis in 1958, the diminutive artist deserves respect and recognition, not only for his ground-breaking fusion of funk and rock, but for his ability constantly to re-invent himself in a variety of pseudonyms and characters throughout his career. Known variously as "Camille", "Alexander Nevermind", "Christopher", "Christopher Trace", "Spooky Electric", "The Kid" and, most recently "Ecnirp", Prince has managed to sustain a pop life coloured with constant creative cloudbursts in which many musical styles have been melded together to create sounds which appear entirely new.

Not only distinguished by his penchant for assuming a range of different personalities, Prince is the only major artist in the world to have produced himself in his recordings from day one as a signed act. A prolific songwriter, Prince is rumoured to have thousands of songs stored in the vaults of his Paisley Park recording complex in his hometown. Furthermore, he has never been slow to put his songwriting abilities to good use, providing songs for a wide range of artists including his protégées Vanity 6 and Appolonia 6, Sheena Easton, Mavis Staples, Chaka Khan and The Bangles. With the latter, Prince was to gain the distinction of being the only US artist to achieve a US number-one single (with "Kiss" in 1986) and have the number-two slot occupied by another of his songs recorded as a cover with The Bangles' version of "Manic Monday".

OPPOSITE, LEFT: **Prince and protégé Sheila E. arriving at Heathrow Airport, London.**

OPPOSITE, TOP LEFT: **Paisley Park studios, where Prince crafts his intricate and individual work.**

FAR LEFT: **Prince resuscitated the career of husky-voiced Mavis Staples, with the powerful 1989 album** *Time Waits for No One*.

RIGHT: **The Purple One on stage in 1988.**

Prince has also made the unlikely bedfellows of sex and God the bedrock of his songwriting career. Taking the lead from the likes of James Brown and Marvin Gaye, he has carved himself a niche in the world of rock music in which his own inimitable synthesis of a wide range of musical styles from jazz and rap to rock and pop has assured him of the continued devotion of an international army of fans.

LEFT: **Prince has written songs for Sheena Easton, Chaka Khan and the Bangles, among many others.**

OPPOSITE: **With a synthesis of styles that includes funk, rap, jazz, rock and pop, Prince is one of the true originals.**

· QUEEN ·

The most educated band in rock are Queen, with three of the four members holding degrees and all having attended college at some time or another. Brian May, the band's guitarist, had been asked by the pre-eminent astronomer Sir Bernard Lovell to work at the Jodrell Bank radio telescope, but chose a life as a rock musician instead, although he continued to work towards a PhD until the band shot into the big time from around 1974 onwards.

Brian May is also unique in that, as far as we can ascertain, he is the only top-flight rock guitarist to wield an instrument made from the remnants of a 19th-century mahogany fireplace.

Much of Queen's early appeal was in the originality of their sound, with voices multi-tracked to epic proportions and the characteristic tone of May's fireplace guitar. Brian May is also the only guitarist to use an old coin as a plectrum, gaining a readily recognizable metallic "scratch" before the note proper, a device which has become almost as distinctive a trademark as Jimi Hendrix's feedback or Eric Clapton's "womantone".

Queen's world-wide success grew from 1975 when the album *Sheer Heart Attack* charted on both sides of the Atlantic and spawned the hit single "Killer Queen". The same year Queen scored another first with what is their best remembered hit "Bohemian Rhapsody". Originally seven minutes long, the track was edited down to five minutes and 52 seconds for public consumption and it topped the UK charts for nine weeks, the longest run on the charts since Paul Anka did the business with "Diana" 18 years before.

Where the record broke truly new ground was with the promotional tactics used. The accompanying video was

ABOVE LEFT: **Queen, shortly after the** formation of the band and prior to the monumental hit, "Bohemian Rhapsody".

ABOVE: **The sadly missed Freddie Mercury on stage with Queen. His death from AIDS in** December 1991 brought to an end two years as a recluse, along with intense media speculation.

directed by Bruce Gower, and although it was not the first film-clip to be used to promote a record, it was the first video and, as such, it heralded a trend within the music industry world-wide, whereby the making of a promotional video became a prerequisite for the most humble of bands' record releases.

Other records fell to the four-piece as their career blossomed throughout the eighties. In 1984, when "Radio Ga Ga" reached number two behind Frankie Goes To Hollywood's "Relax", they became the only group in history to have had four top-10 hits each written by individual members of the group. They are also one of the few modern rock groups to have enjoyed a stint on the UN cultural blacklist after their well-received but ideologically unsound shows at South Africa's Sun City.

ABOVE: Queen grew out of the art school band Smile, which the Zanzibar-born Mercury formed in the early seventies.

BELOW: Brian May, whose guitar is made from a mahogany fireplace, achieves his distinctive sound by using a coin as a plectrum.

Queen have always treated the live side of their work as distinctly separate from their studio recording, and their live sets have set records of their own – not least is the fact that Queen were the first Western band to have a concert filmed behind the now-defunct "Iron Curtain" when they played in Budapest, Hungary in 1986. Queen also hold the awesome record of being the band (as opposed to billed, single artist) to have played to the biggest number of paying customers when their gig in São Paulo, Brazil, attracted a staggering 231,000 fans.

For two years, there was intense speculation in the media about Freddie Mercury's disappearance from the public eye. The rumours ended when, in December 1991, after a short written announcement, he died of AIDS.

RIOTS

The danger presumed to be inherent in rock 'n' roll has resulted on many occasions in what the forces of law and order would term a riot.

The early live appearances by Elvis Presley in the southern states of America in the mid-fifties provoked excited reactions among audiences unused to the singer's blatant use of sexuality in his performance. It was not until later, with the release of the films *Blackboard Jungle* and *Rock Around The Clock*, in Great Britain that rock 'n' roll was to hit the headlines for the first time as the catalyst to scenes of violent disorder among the young audiences.

The breaking-up of a few cinema seats in quiet towns up and down the British Isles paled into insignificance with the annual running battles held at seaside resorts during the sixties. Rival gangs of Mods and Rockers, each with an allegiance to a particular lifestyle, underpinned by definite and opposite musical tastes, played out their aggressively male battle fantasies on the holiday beaches. Although these riots were sensationally reported in the newsreels and press of the day, and offenders were heavily penalized in the courts, there were surprisingly few serious injuries and, happily, no fatalities.

The Rolling Stones, in their capacity as headline act at what was to become the infamous Altamont festival held in San Francisco in December 1969, witnessed unprecedented violence at the site – the speedway track at Allamende County, California. The local chapter of Hell's Angels had been engaged to police the event for payment of $500 worth of beer.

The opening set by Santana saw the Angels embark on an ostentatious display of power and aggression by constantly moving through the crowd, onto the stage and back again, ignoring the music in favour of exercising and enjoying a rare opportunity for legitimate, sanctioned crowd control. By the time Jefferson Airplane took the stage, the atmosphere at the event had degenerated, with the Angels apparently in total control of the site. Marty Balin of Airplane attempted to dissuade an over-zealous Angel from meting out a beating to a hapless fan by addressing the "security man" from the stage. This resulted in another Angel beating Balin to the ground with a pool cue in a witty rebuttal of his request. The other members of the band played on.

The Rolling Stones did not appear onstage until after dark. Some felt that the band were attempting to allow the rapidly worsening situation to calm itself down, others believed that Jagger, who had also been on the receiving end of some "advice" from the beery stewards, was waiting until dark to heighten the anticipation

and subsequent impact of the Stones' arrival onstage. Surrounded by a phalanx of Hell's Angels, many of whom were seen to jeer the performance, the band launched into "Sympathy for the Devil". It soon became apparent that there was a major disturbance underway only yards from the stage. The full horror of those fleeting minutes was captured by the cameras filming the set for the planned feature *Gimme Shelter*. A young black man named Meredith Hunter can be seen in the resulting footage. He runs through the crowd chased by an Angel who succeeds in stabbing the fleeing fan in the back. Hunter turns and, in full view of the cameras, pulls a gun. Instantly, he is surrounded by a mob of Angels and is repeatedly stabbed until he dies.

Although no strangers to riotous scenes and the odd bout of violence – the band had had shows halted by riot police in 1964 in The Hague and in Paris – the death at Altamont tainted the utopian ideals of the time and introduced violence of a kind never before seen to the world of rock. It was as if rock 'n' roll had somehow aged and grown ugly overnight.

ABOVE: **Riots and protests dogged the Sex Pistols' tour of the USA in 1978.**

The Rolling Stones enjoy a similar status to vinyl 45s in the history of rock music; it's hard to imagine how things would have been without them.

The last few years have seen the Stones roll on while young pretenders borrow liberally from their attitude, their moves, their licks and their lifestyle. British band the Soup Dragons with a reworking of the Stones "I'm Free . . ." and Scottish rockers Primal Scream recently engaged the services of ex-Stones' producer Jimmy Miller to re-create the vibe and the sound of the Stones' late sixties sessions. But as the Stones edge collectively towards respectable middle age, and despite the other Stones' plea to Jagger to "stop acting like Peter Pan and grow up",

interest in the band shows no sign of abating. For example, their 1989 Steel Wheels tour grossed a phenomenal $100 million – a world record for any tour, anywhere, to date.

For parents, a Stones record or show is something which takes them back to the sixties or seventies when the Stones were at their peak. For the young the Stones provide authentic material upon which to base their own reworkings of the sixties' raga-rock sound and the seventies' R 'n' B.

The Stones are able to boast that they are the longest-serving rock band ever to emerge from the shores of the UK. The group was created in the offices of manager Andrew Oldham (an ex-Beatles PR man) on 1 May 1963, although the

ABOVE: **A value-for-money bill in the UK, 1963.**

TOP: **Mick Jagger transformed the Stones' 1969 free concert in Hyde Park into a memorial service for the just drowned Brian Jones – he quoted Shelley and released several thousand butterflies.**

OPPOSITE: **The Stones' new boy, Ronnie Wood, has only 16 years of membership behind him. He quit the Faces to replace Mick Taylor during the Stones' 1975 US tour.**

band had been playing together as Blues Incorporated and The Rollin' Stones for several months. Although some have accused the band of tagging on to the coat-tails of The Beatles during the 1960s – recording songs written by Lennon and McCartney ("I Wanna Be Your Man") and following the Fabs to India in 1967 – the truth is that early on, the Stones developed a highly distinctive approach to their music and with it, gained fans of a type dissimilar to the average Beatles devotee.

The Rolling Stones' roots were always in R 'n' B, and all of their releases from "Come On", in 1963, onwards demonstrated a healthy respect and a love for that particular strand of music. While The Beatles were mainly playing on their vocal talents and making the most of their fascination with the melodies of Buddy Holly, the Everley's and the other early rockers, the Stones were crafting a hard-driving R 'n' B style. Witness their toughening-up of the Beatles' Ringo vehicle "I Wanna Be Your Man" or their melding of Buddy Holly and Bo Diddley on "Not Fade Away". The early Stones swiftly established a reputation for cavemen-like rhythms and, with their long hair, they were often characterized by the mainstream press as a threatening, alien and dark presence on the pop scene – in opposition to The Beatles, who were every mother's son image.

Jagger, as frontman, early on developed a vocal style which owed more to the Mississippi delta than his home town of Dartford in England, and a stage presence owing more to the bedroom than the live venue.

The Stones stuck closely to their R 'n' B roots until the mid-sixties when flirtations with hallucinogenic drugs helped to spawn a new version of the band. Thankfully, many of the band's fans were also exploring the possibilities afforded by recreational chemicals and so the new music, a kind of R 'n' B-tinged, Indian-influenced rock 'n' roll found a ready audience.

The Stones have the honour of being the first band ever to flaunt an association with the occult and with devil worship with their 1968 *Satanic Majesties* set. Delivered to the shops in a

flashy three-dimensional sleeve, the album alienated some but delighted many. The belated contribution to psychedelia that was *Satanic Majesties* signalled the beginning of an era of change and upheaval of the Stones. Dogged by the police for their, by now, acknowledged use of drugs, the Stones were to lose Brian Jones in a tragic accident in July 1969. In December of that year, the group gained yet more notoriety and a hefty £375,000 lawsuit from the owners of the Altamont site at which a killing in the crowd at the Stones' free concert had further darkened the group's public image.

In spite, or perhaps because, of these upheavals the group seemed to find a stronger direction after the meanderings of *Satanic Majesties*. "Honky Tonk Woman" spent five weeks at the top of the UK charts in 1969 and represented for many a return to the kind of form, and not least the musical roots, which had characterized the Stones at their best.

The seventies saw the Stones consolidate their position as a live rock

'n' roll band *par excellence* with the albums *Get Yer Ya Ya's Out, Sticky Fingers* and the live side of *Gimme Shelter*. The double *Exile On Main Street* remains something of a classic. Although it is as a live act that the Stones

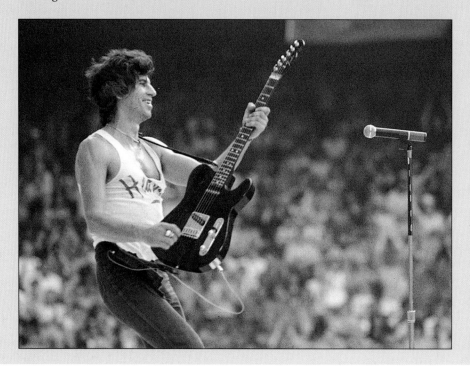

have continued to find favour with audiences all over the world, their 28-year career has also spawned 31 top-10 US LPs (a record), 27 top-10 UK albums (a record) and 33 gold and 15 platinum albums in total. Not bad!

LEFT: **Mick Jagger's frontman talents have seen him through over three decades at the top.**

OPPOSITE, LEFT: **Keith Richard on stage in Belgium in 1988. The Stones' reputation as "the greatest rock 'n' roll band in the world" is sustained by their live act.**

OPPOSITE, TOP LEFT: **The Rolling Stones bandwagon hits Philadelphia during their 1989 Steel Wheels tour.**

SUPERGROUPS

The first sighting of the uncommon but none-too-rare rock phenomenon, the supergroup, came in 1957 at that most sacred of sonic sites, Sam Phillips' Sun studios on Union Avenue, Memphis, Tennessee.

Elvis Presley, while on a seasonal winter break from recording tracks for his new label RCA, paid a surprise visit to the scene of his first recording sessions. That very day a session was taking place with Carl Perkins, writer of the classic "Blue Suede Shoes", featuring Jerry Lee Lewis on piano. Also in attendance was country legend Johnny Cash, and it was with these three that Presley spent an afternoon "jamming" around various standards. Two versions of the traditional "Peace In The Valley" were laid to tape, and the session, unreleased until some years after Presley's death, entered rock 'n' roll history, with what was undoubtedly the first, albeit ad hoc, supergroup, which became known as The Million Dollar Quartet.

Eric Clapton, given the nickname "God" by adoring disciples of his discs in the mid-sixties, holds the record for being the only world-famous musician to have made a career out of supergroups. With his involvement in the line-ups of The Yardbirds and John Mayall's Bluesbreakers, he established a reputation for excessive expertise on the electric guitar. With the formation of

Cream with bassist Jack Bruce and drummer Ginger Baker in 1966, Clapton began a long list of associations with other musicians of his own calibre. After Cream came Blind Faith with Stevie Winwood, followed by Derek and the Dominoes with Duane Allman. Clapton also formed the nucleus of the Plastic Ono band with John Lennon, drummer Alan White and bassist Klaus

ABOVE: **Mark Knopfler, who has spread his talents around with the likes of Bob Dylan and the Notting Hillbillies, here leads another rock collective.**

Voorman, and played with George Harrison in the band assembled for the Concert for Bangladesh and Harrison's album *All Things Must Pass*, which featured Leon Russell, Ringo Starr, Klaus Voorman, Billy Preston and Jim Keltner.

Although initially gathered together for nothing more than an extensive jam, the "rockestra" formed by Paul McCartney for his set at the Concerts for the People of Kampuchea held at London's Hammersmith Odeon in December 1979, holds the record for being the biggest supergroup in terms of numbers of famous musicians taking part in one specifically written song. Apart from the marvellous McCartney and his singing spouse Linda, the group included members of most of the bands who had appeared in the concerts over the previous days.

"Lucky" Dylan, George "Nelson" Harrison, Jeff "Otis" Lynne, Roy "Lefty" Orbison and Tom "Charlie T Jnr" Petty joined forces in 1988 to become the Traveling Wilburys. This unlikely, though hugely popular, supergroup grew out of an informal gathering at Tom Petty's house, where the five giants of three decades of rock went back to their roots, rediscovered their initial enthusiasm and, quite literally, became a garage band. The resulting first album, imaginatively entitled *The Traveling Wilburys Volume One*, was a world-wide best seller, a consequence of which was the revitalization of the Big O's career. But his untimely death in November of that year led to the group's second album, the arrival of which was heavily hinted at in the title of the first, not featuring Orbison at all.

SAMPLING

magine the convenience of being able to reproduce perfectly any given sound in crisply defined studio stereo. When, in 1966, John Lennon asked producer George Martin to supply the sound of a thousand chanting Buddhist monks for the outro of "Tomorrow Never Knows" on the album *Revolver*, little did he know that one day, only 20 years later, his request would have been realized within minutes due to the eclectic electronics of the sampler. The advance in digital technology since the early eighties led to the development of a machine the like of which had never been seen before. Now musicians could not only steal a tune but also the sounds and performances that other producers and players had laboured over for a considerable period of time. Sampling allows a "sound-bite" to be lifted from any source and then manipulated and sculpted at will.

The first applications of the new technique were to be found in the dance sector, where producers working on tight budgets and in small studios required a greater range of sounds than their meagre resources otherwise would permit. The first rock hit single fully to feature the technique was "E=Mc^2" by Big Audio Dynamite in 1986. It was the second single from ex-Clash guitarist Mick Jones' new percussion-based group, and their biggest hit to date.

The record for most sampled artist must surely be awarded to Georgia Jailbird, the Godfather of Soul. The hardest-working man in showbusiness, ladies and gentlemen, we give you, James Brown's drummer. The un-named skin-basher who belted out the sublime beat to Brown's "Funky Drummer", originally a hit in the US in 1970, has won untold fame and, we wager, very little money by being used on a plethora of house, rap and indie-dance crossover records in the last three years.

BOTTOM: **Ex-Clash guitarist Mick Jones and his group Big Audio Dynamite had the first rock hit to feature samples with "E=MC^2" in 1986.**

BELOW: **The ending of the Beatles' "Tomorrow Never Knows" includes George Martin's sample of a thousand chanting Buddhist monks.**

· STATUS QUO ·

Status Quo have been around for longer than most British bands, having emerged in 1967. Although their success was never to cross the Atlantic, the group has enjoyed a large degree of recognition in most of the world's territories, including Australia and Europe.

It is in terms of UK chart successes, however, that the band holds the records. With 40 consecutive chart-entry singles the band are now ahead of their nearest rivals, the Rolling Stones, by six and the next down are the Hollies with 31.

Not content with that particular

ABOVE: **Status Quo in the heads-down-no-nonsense-boogie stance that revived their career. The band had an unbroken run of 32 Top 40 hits in the UK, a feat no other group can boast.**

RIGHT: **The early Quo were purveyors of psychedelic bubble-gum music and scored two top-10 hits before becoming disenchanted with their pop image.**

record, The Quo embarked upon a stunt in September 1991 under the banner Rock Till You Drop. The idea was to play a complete UK tour in 24 hours, playing full sets at four major venues across the UK, rushing to the next gig in a combination of fast cars and helicopters. The successful completion of

the tour has assured the group a place in the official record books, that is until someone else dreams up and completes a similar breath-taking rock 'n' roll feat.

TOURING

ost of the overnight successes, those sudden flarings of supernovae in the otherwise inky celestial firmament of pop, and the hyped-up hitmaking hipsters, all without exception, know the tediousness of touring.

The early sixties saw a succession of star-studded showcases, bills made of fatigued but increasingly famous faces who quite literally took their music "on the road". The mid-fifties saw American promoter and DJ Alan Freed, who reputedly coined the term "rock and roll", present the first "package" tours. His 1958 outing, modestly entitled Alan Freed's Big Beat Show, played over 60 dates with a line-up including Chuck Berry, Buddy Holly and the Crickets, Jerry Lee Lewis, Frankie Lymon, and Danny and the Juniors. Value for money and make no mistake!

In the UK, entrepreneur Larry Parnes, known to his friends as "Mr Parnes, Shillings and Pence", introduced the idea of touring with a string of stupendous and star-studded revues. The cream of Britain's beat-boom bands were included in Parnes' line-ups but his most famous achievement was hiring The Beatles for their first fully fledged tour. The group, known then as the Silver Beetles, failed an audition to back Parnes' main attraction, Billy Fury, but gained the dubious prize of becoming the back-up band for fellow-Parnes' artiste Johnny Gentle, on his 1960 seven-day tour of Scotland.

By the mid-seventies stadium-sized tours had become a lucrative undertaking for many successful acts. Along with associated merchandising and live records, the revenue generated made tours lasting years, rather than weeks, the norm. In record-breaking terms, the nature of touring as it has developed over the last 20 years means that the scale of tours is constantly growing. Attendance figures, revenue generated, countries visited and the lengths of the tours themselves are all exponentially expanding.

With the avid interest in witnessing the spectacle of live rock performances having shown no sign of abating, the logistics of putting a show on the road have had to develop in order to cope with audience demand. At one end of the scale, the sweaty club is still the favoured venue for experiencing rock at its best but, at the other end, the growth of communicative media and the very technology of amplification and lighting has allowed vast stadia to become the favoured setting for the extravaganzas mounted by the likes of Pink Floyd, Van Halen, Paul McCartney, Dire Straits, Guns 'n' Roses and many other major-league rock stars.

Such is the size of these undertakings that it is not unusual for two or even three crews to be out on the road at any one time, with whole convoys of articulated trucks travelling "leap-frog" style between venues. Thus, while a band is sound-checking for a show, several tons of identical equipment is being dismantled and sent ahead to be erected for the next performance. Huge computer-controlled lighting rigs and stages, 30,000 watt PA systems, sound technicians, caterers,

ABOVE AND RIGHT:
Alan Freed, reputedly responsible for coining the phrase "rock 'n' roll", was the leading light behind bringing black-based music to middle America.

the sales of tickets for the events themselves, but rely instead on the secondary, but none the less huge income generated from the sale of programmes and other merchandise such as official tour clothing. The subsequent record sales are, of course, the primary reason for embarking on these treks – it's rare, these days, to find a band touring without a record to promote.

In 1991, Guns 'n' Roses embarked on a record-breaking round-the-world trip, playing shows in 23 nations over a 30-month period. This massive, money-spinning tour is expected to earn the individual members in excess of $15 million each.

The oddly named Lollapalooza tour put together by Jane's Addiction singer Perry Farrel in 1991 is also worthy of mention. After an aborted appearance at the previous year's Reading Festival in England, Farrel hit upon the idea of taking a similarly inspired line-up across the US in a multi-media package extravaganza. The bill included Jane's Addiction, Nine Inch Nails, Siouxsie and the Banshees, and gangsta giant Ice T.

road crew, security, merchandising and management, film crews, pilots for the bands' helicopters, drivers for the limousines and trucks, hairdressers, masseurs and physiotherapists, scaffold riggers, pyrotechnics and special effects experts – any or all of these can be found working on a modern large-scale tour.

Bands now know how to swing the huge touring machine into operation with comparative ease, but at great expense – many tours make little or no money on

TASTELESSNESS

Rock 'n' roll has never prided itself upon its ability to remain within the bounds of good taste. Indeed, it has been at times, a prerequisite of commercial success to cross the boundaries laid down by the self-designated right-thinking majority in pursuit of a rock 'n' roll lifestyle which, when carefully publicized, will attract and hold the attention of the waiting public.

The most flagrant crossing of the imaginary boundary between good and bad taste occurred in 1965 when The Beatles, who had been enjoying their status as the band that everyone's grandmother liked, outraged and alienated a huge section of their American audience with John Lennon's famous and often misquoted remark about the band being more popular than Jesus Christ. Lennon actually commented on the obvious renunciation of the Christian faith all over the world, stating: "Christianity will go, it will vanish and shrink. I needn't argue about that; I'm right and I will be proved right. We're more popular than Jesus now – I don't know which will go first, Christianity or rock and roll."

Taken out of context by the press and castigated for his apparent godless arrogance, ultimately and unfairly, Lennon was forced to apologize for the remarks. The respite from public condemnation was, however, brief. It seemed as though the band had moved in an instant from their status as everybody's favourite to simply a British band who had got too big for their boots and had taken it upon themselves to offend the American public.

Other performers have based their entire careers on an obvious and highly entertaining form of bad taste. The most notable of these is Alice Cooper, whose antics with corpses, chickens, snakes, guillotines, executioners and giant dentist's drills led to all manner of macabre machinations. The million-selling album *Billion Dollar Babies* released at the pinnacle of Cooper's popularity in 1973 contained such questionable and highly diverting songs as "Sick Things" and the epic "I Love the Dead". The inclusion of such titles in no way helped the sales of the album. Or did they?

The only musical movement to be founded entirely upon its desire to shock and outrage "normal" people was punk. The explosion of energetic music centred

RIGHT: **Since 1970, Alice Cooper has masterminded the most bizarre stage show, incorporating masochism, sadism, self-abuse, murder,** suicide and general degeneracy, in the history of rock. Meanwhile, he wrote catchy songs, such as "School's Out" and "I'm Eighteen".

lesser degree those of his fans when he bit the head off of a live bat while onstage. Obnoxious Ozzy later said that he thought the large-eared, poorly sighted creature was a rubber fake, thrown onto the stage by a like-minded fan.

Others who have found themselves on the wrong side of the line between public decency and indecency include Madonna, who found herself castigated by the Catholic Church while on tour in Italy with the Blonde Ambition package in 1990, for allegedly making light of the symbolism and sacraments of the Mass. The Church called unsuccessfully for her show to be banned. She was in good company: Detroit burned the Beatles' records, Britain banned the Sex Pistols, and NBC banned Elvis – all on the grounds of public decency, or taste. It would almost seem that to be seen to lack taste is something of a badge of rock 'n' roll legitimacy.

ABOVE:
Originally with heavy metal band Black Sabbath, Ozzy Osbourne literally had a bad taste!

RIGHT: **Sid Vicious, middle class white boy from suburban England, turned into the ultimate rock music anti-hero, when he joined Sex Pistols as bassist.**

around London, England in 1976-7 relied upon the use of an iconography which had as little to do with accepted notions of taste as possible. The convention of spitting at punk bands was seized upon by fans as a desirable replacement for polite applause, while dress was a combination of do-it-yourself ripped and painted clothing, or store-bought bondage clothing, dog collars and the ubiquitous leather biker's jacket. Bizarre and unconventional facial make up for men and women complemented the look. The impact of the punk was due to the nihilistic, anti-establishment stance coupled with the use of clothes and a music which initially defied convention. However, all such movements are eventually subsumed into mainstream culture and so cease to be seen as a threat to public taste and decency.

The rotund Birmingham barnstormer Ozzy Osbourne quite literally left a bad taste in his own mouth and to a

· TALKING HEADS ·

anking alongside Queen as one of the most educated bands in rock, Talking Heads began their life in 1974 and rode the crest of the new wave in New York before taking their brand of quirky, arty rock on the road.

The classic single "Psycho Killer" set the tone for their style in the late seventies when the band became inextricably linked with the punk and new wave scene on both sides of the Atlantic, proving that the writing and recording of music that was innovative and challenging did not have to consist of three minutes of white noise.

Talking Heads enter the record books for a characteristically odd reason. On the 1984 film of the concert called *Stop Making Sense*, Scots-born David Byrne wore the most enormous and ill-fitting suit ever seen on a rock stage during a live performance. Eclipsing the baggyness of even Little Richard's in his heyday, Byrne's large white suit was so huge that he was able to dance inside of the jacket and trousers without the suit moving at all.

RIGHT: Talking Heads' early music incorporated a memorable mixture of quirky wit, raw new wave excitement and driving urban funk.

FAR RIGHT TOP: David Byrne's stick insect physique is swamped inside the famous *Stop Making Sense* baggy suit.

ABOVE: The seminal *Talking Heads 77*, which features their best-known single, the classic "Psycho Killer".

The Irish people have a long history of artistry in the traditional use of lilting lyricism, as well as not charging income tax to those fortunate enough to be able to prove their professional status as an "artist".

The eighties saw a surprising rise in the fortunes of the Emerald Isle in terms of musical impact on the world of rock. Bob Geldof's masterminding of Live Aid saw him become a statesman-like figure world-wide, but it was the inexorable rise of Dublin rockers U2 which made Ireland a musical fountainhead to be reckoned with.

U2 were formed in 1976 in Dublin while Bono, The Edge, Adam Clayton and Larry Mullen were all at school together. They set the pattern for their subsequent world-wide success with their first number one in their native country, an EP released on CBS Ireland called "Out of Control". Crossing the Irish Sea the following year secured a recording deal with Chris Blackwell's independent Island Records and the rest, as they say, is history.

The rise of U2 to star-status on a world-wide basis was underlined by the group's achievement with what was to become the most successful live album release ever, *Under A Blood Red Sky* in 1983. A mere four years later, *The Joshua Tree* entered the UK chart at number one. The album achieved platinum status within 48 hours of its release and is the fastest-selling album in UK chart history. *Rattle and Hum,* the band's soundtrack to their filmed record of their American tour of 1988, was a further multi-million seller, and went some way to establishing the often-repeated assertion by fans of the band that U2 are "the greatest rock 'n' roll band in the world" – followers of the Stones, Guns 'n' Roses or even Primal Scream might, however, disagree.

LEFT: **The 1983 release *Under a Blood Red Sky* is the most successful live album of all time.**

ABOVE: **Much of U2's early success was due to live shows and live albums.**

VINYL

It is difficult to imagine rock 'n' roll without the vinyl record; in its unthinkable absence just how would the music have had the impact it did? Early records were 10-inch, 78-revolutions-per-minute items made from a curious substance known as shellac. This material was rather unusual in that it was made from the secretions of *Coccus lacca*, the tiny Indian lac beetle. Dried shellac is unfortunately rather brittle, and was subsequently responsible for a great number of broken records in the forties and fifties.

The developments in thermoplastics which led to the introduction to the world of mass-produced nylon, also enabled the manufacture of polyvinylchloride, better known as PVC. Although Emile Berliner had invented the recorded disc in 1896, it was not until the potential of vinyl, with its malleability and storage capability, that microgroove technology became possible.

These advances made it possible to attain greater fidelity in the reproduction of sound by packing more information into a record's groove on a more durable, slower-revolving disc. Instead of 78, the new standard speeds of 33⅓ or 33.33rpm for a 12-inch-long player and 45rpm for a 7-inch single were fairly arbitrary choices, but quickly established themselves as world standards.

With the burgeoning boom in rock 'n' roll, the vinyl junky was born. The medium became popular with an underground *cognoscenti* whose knowledge of different labels and their releases, rare imports and deletions, and more importantly how to find these desirable discs, set the pattern for an all-consuming hobby that carries on to this day.

Sales of vinyl in the late fifties and early sixties were an indicator for the record-breaking consumer boom of the time. Sales of singles in particular were then at an all-time high, with million-selling 7-inchers being a regular occurrence.

The first threat to the pre-eminence of the polymer platter was when tape crossed over from the recording studio into the domestic arena. The Dutch-based electronics giant Phillips took the initiative and introduced the "compact cassette" in the late sixties. The idea was embraced by industry and consumer alike, with the emergent Japanese audio manufacturers adopting it as a standard format. With the advantage of being playable at home, in the car, and later with the introduction of the "Walkman", literally anywhere, cassette sales rocketed through the seventies, and at the end of that decade finally rivalled vinyl discs as the most preferred musical medium.

The Sex Pistols' manager and *agent provocateur* Malcolm McClaren, always at the forefront of events, in this case can rightly claim a worldwide first. With his protégées Bow Wow Wow, he released the first commercially available cassette-only single with the 1981 "Your Cassette Pet", featuring the prophetic paeon "C30, C60, C90 Go".

Throughout the eighties cassette sales consistently outstripped those of vinyl, with many releases in the USA not even feturing a plastic disc format. In 1989, Swedish songsters Roxette gained the accolade of being the first artists to have a number-one single in the States with the track "Listen To Your Heart" released on cassette format only.

The item that could signal the death of vinyl records is the Compact Disc. Developed from the early eighties onwards in Europe and Japan, the CD is as different from a vinyl record as black is from white. Technology once again played its hand, with cheap lasers and micro-circuits enabling computer-derived digital audio to appear in a domestic setting.

The popularity of the CD has been underlined by the willingness of the public to invest in the new technology, and the first album to sell a million copies in CD format

OPPOSITE, FAR LEFT: "C30, C60, C90, Go!" sang Annabella of Bow Wow Wow when they released the first cassette-only single through a major record company in 1981.

ABOVE: Swedish rockers Roxette claimed the first number one US chart single with a cassette-only release: "Listen to Your Heart".

LEFT: *Brothers In Arms* by Dire Straits was the first CD to notch up a million sales.

– despite being available on conventional cassettes and LPs – was Dire Straits' 1985 set *Brothers in Arms*.

The artist has taken the CD to heart because it enables the listener to hear a near-perfect reproduction of the studio sound, and the industry loves the CD because it can sell to fans new copies of those worn, played-out favourite albums in a brand-new format. Brand-new, that is, until the industry comes up with something to replace CDs. We wonder what DAT will be?

· VAN HALEN ·

With their first album *Van Halen* selling over 2 million copies and the follow-up, the imaginatively titled Van Halen 2 selling over 5 million, the band found themselves riding a wave of massive popularity as the 1980s got underway.

Building their reputation as a live band required a good deal of trucking knowledge as their on-the-road equipment weighed in at a staggering 22 tons. Never known as a group to run shy of the flamboyant entrance, Van Halen have the distinction of being the only band to have hired lookalikes to parachute in to the beginning of a gig. The Vans sealed their reputation as a live act to be respected if not hired on a whim, when they were paid $1 million for a single appearance at the second US Festival at San Bernadino in May 1983. It was the biggest fee ever payed for a single performance.

Guitarist Eddie van Halen not only gave his name to the group but gave a new guitar style to the world. He was the first to introduce and perfect the combination of whammy-bar and neck-mounted transducer to create solos of apparently unplayable speed, unpredictability and diversity as heard on Michael Jackson's "Beat It" in 1983.

Although vocalist and frontman David Lee Roth left the group in 1985, Van Halen soldiered on with replacement Sammy Hagar and, in 1988, took part in the Monsters of Rock tour which also featured The Scorpions, Kingdom Come, Metallica, and Dokken. The tour was the most ambitious heavy metal jaunt yet to be undertaken, with 250,000 watts of sound on 20 all-day festival gigs.

RIGHT: **Van Halen on the Monsters of Rock tour.**

LEFT: **Eddie Van Halen's guitar solo helped Michael Jackson's "Beat It" to reach a wide crossover audience in 1983.**

INSET: **David Lee Roth left Van Halen to pursue a solo career.**

· THE WHO ·

In west London in the early sixties, the movement known as "mod" saw teenagers squandering their hard-earned cash on expensive Italian clothes, shoes, hairstyles and motor-scooters. With their musical appetites stimulated by imported US soul and R 'n' B, it did not take very long for musically minded mods to hook up with enterprising entrepreneurs to form home-grown mod groups with built-in appeal for the three-buttoned, five-inch-vented, mohair-suited, amphetamine-fuelled underground groovers, The Mods.

So it was that The Who, later dubbed The High Numbers and then, finally, The Who again, began making their characteristic racket around the pubs and clubs of Shepherd's Bush, London. They were the first group to own the

means of producing their music, and then systematically destroy it at every available opportunity. Their ritual abuse of guitars, drum kits and amplification was seen as the perfect, pop-art expression of repressed anger and rebellion by their fans, while detractors of the group claimed that these destructive tendencies were nothing more than hyped-up showmanship. Whatever the case, the band were the first to make the trashing of equipment a regular feature of their live performance.

The Who emerged during the sixties' beatboom as the perfect export from London, the centre of all that was swinging in the mid-sixties, and their explosive entry to the US, clad in the Union Jack, capitalized upon The Beatles' earlier success.

As well as being the first group to use feedback on a chart single in 1964 with "Anytime Anyhow Anywhere", The Who were also the first to dabble with the idea of the "concept" album. The 1966 release of the long-player *A Quick One While He's Away* featured a track of the same title which took up the whole of one side of the album.

Perhaps the most important first for Townshend and his colleagues was in producing the very first commercially successful rock opera. Although not the first of its kind (that dubious distinction goes to The Pretty Things with their *SF Sorrow*), *Tommy*, released in 1969, won generous praise from critics and fans alike and eventually spawned a film which starred The Who's corkscrew-haired singer Roger Daltrey. It also gave The Who the opportunity to be the first rock band to play the prestigious Metropolitan Opera House in New York City.

The band also has a well-deserved reputation for volume, and their performance at the Isle of Wight festival in 1969 used one of the largest PA systems ever constructed in the UK. Such was the potential for damage to the eardrums of the spectators, that signs

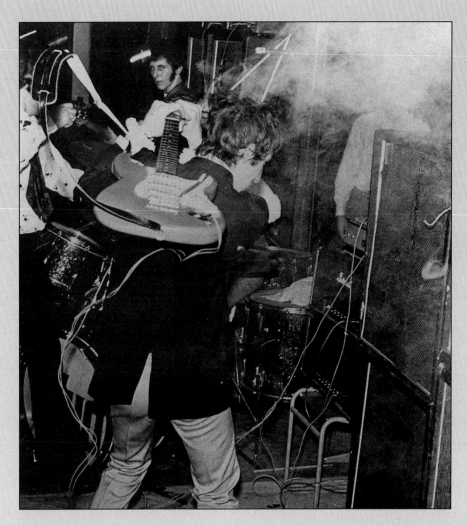

were hung upon the speaker cabs warning the already deafened masses not to come within 15 feet of the stacks.

The Who consolidated their position as the official "loudest band in the world" with their performance at Charlton Athletic Football Stadium, East London, in 1976.

OPPOSITE, TOP LEFT: The Who in 1966, two years before their triumphant appearance at Woodstock. The mod image adopted by the group became a key fashion style for the emergent "Swinging London" scene.

TOP: Pete Townshend vents some pent-up pop-art anger on a Fender Stratocaster.

RIGHT: The Who in 1988, with drummer Keith Moon's replacement Kenny Jones (third from left).

WOODSTOCK

The Woodstock Music and Arts Fair: An Aquarian Exposition was the full title of the event which saw the third-largest city in New York State grow up overnight on one August weekend in 1969. Peopled in part by the new generation of flower-children, born of the Summer of Love and nurtured over the succeeding two years on a diet of peace, love and psychedelia, the city was albeit a short-lived community of like minds.

As an example of the underground counter-culture, the festival was sustained, surprisingly, by the old capitalist trick of throwing money at the problems arising from the decision to stage the event. The original $500,000 budget was quickly exceeded before any acts were booked.

The projected problem of purloining performers was yet to be overcome. However, the method by which the stars were eventually lured to perform in a field in front of the great unwashed was arrived at after small deliberation: pay them inordinately large amounts of money. The first to sign up were Creedence Clearwater Revival, who agreed to perform a set for the then enourmous amount of $10,000. Other artists were soon to follow.

With only a month to go before the fabled Aquarian Exposition, a small problem remained: there was no definite site agreed on which the event could take place. At this point, a dairy farmer from Bethel in upstate New York made himself a lot of money and became a folk hero at the same time by agreeing to allow the festival

ABOVE: Jefferson Airplane, along with the Grateful Dead, was the most creative, prolific and long-lasting of the groups to emerge from Haight-Ashbury, LA, in the late sixties.

BELOW RIGHT: Arlo Guthrie, son of Bob Dylan's mentor Woody, began recording his own music in 1967. Prior to Woodstock, he made his name with the song "Alice's Restaurant".

to take place on his land at Woodstock. The man's name was Max Yasgur.

When the event finally got under way on Friday, 15 August, the profit motive had been altruistically abandoned. The policeman in charge of security intended his campaign to consist entirely of passive policing, and so the fence that was to have been the boundary of the festival was never erected. Its place was taken by a string of stewards who asked people to pay as they arrived to see the performances.

"Woodstock", as the event came to be known to all and sundry, subsequently generated the film and two double albums which featured many, if not all, of the personalities and bands to be found in trhe short-lived "City of Love".

Artists flown in for the delectation of their spaced-out audience included Joan Baez, the Band, Blood Sweat and Tears, the Butterfield Blues Band, Canned Heat, Joe Cocker, Country Joe and the Fish, Creedence Clearwater Revival, Crosby Stills and Nash, The Grateful Dead, Arlo Guthrie, Richie Havens, Jimi Hendrix, The Incredible String Band, Jefferson Airplane, Janis Joplin, Melanie, Santana, Sha-Na-Na, Ravi Shankar, Sly and the Family Stone, Ten Years After, and finally The Who.

Max Yasgur himself summed up the weekend's events from the stage: "This is the largest group ever to have assembled in one place ... I think you people have proven something to the world, that half a million kids can get together and have fun and music and nothing but fun and music."

· XTC ·

There is only one band worthy of any note whose name begins with the letter "X" – that band is XTC. They enter this record book on that achievement alone, as the band (producers of great pop though they surely are) have failed to crack any other records, except in the uniqueness of the initial letter of their collective name.

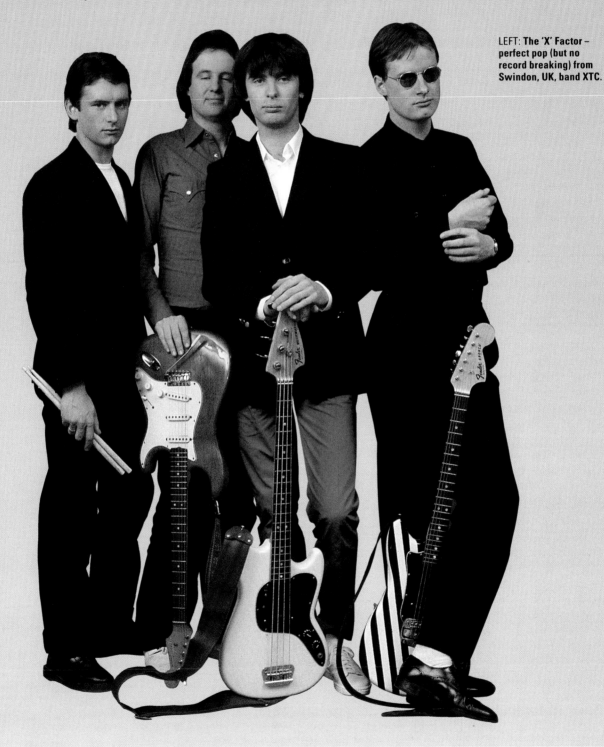

LEFT: **The 'X' Factor – perfect pop (but no record breaking) from Swindon, UK, band XTC.**

The season of goodwill to all men means a great deal to those involved in the music industry – a great deal of money, that is. Ever since Bing Crosby recorded "White Christmas" for the film *Holiday Inn* in 1942, and its subsequent entry into the holly-bedecked halls of fame as the biggest-selling record of all time, the Christmas single has become a tradition endured rather than enjoyed by pop music *aficionados* the world over.

The early rockers quickly got in on the act, with Chuck Berry's version of "Run Run Rudolph" setting an historical precedent for later attempts by the likes of Keith Richards and Brinsley Schwarz.

The religious flavour of some of the finest work the King ever commited to tape was to the festive fore on his 1957 release *Elvis' Christmas Album*. One side of the set featured secular songs along the lines of "Blue Christmas", the similarly titled "White Christmas" and the imaginatively titled "Santa Bring My Baby Back (To Me)". The other side gave Elvis the opportunity to give glorious voice to his gospel heritage. The album was at number one in the US charts for four weeks, and subsequent annual re-promotions led it to sell over one million copies. The set was also made a somewhat cynical cash-in record-breaker by including a 10-page booklet of photographs of the King, thereby giving it that extra gift-giving appeal.

Phil Spector rates a mention for his own contribution to Santa's essential sonic shopping list with his collection *Phil Spector's Christmas Album*, featuring many of his successful stable singing such seasonal standards as "Winter Wonderland", "Rudolph The Red-Nosed Reindeer", and "Santa Claus Is Coming To Town".

Paul McCartney's "Mull of Kintyre", although not officially a Christmas song, leant heavily on a mawkish seasonal sentimentality, and became a massive Christmas hit over a nine-week period in 1977. It went on to become the UK's biggest-selling single, a record it held for the next seven years. McCartney was usurped from this record-breaking position by yet another Christmas release. In 1984 Band Aid's "Do They Know It's Christmas?" topped the charts and became the UK's biggest-selling single to date. The line-up for the record that was to spawn the Live Aid extravaganza included Sting, George Michael, Bono, Bananarama, Phil Collins, Culture Club, Duran Duran, Heaven 17, Kool and the Gang, Spandau Ballet, Status Quo, Paul Weller, Paul Young, and writers Bob Geldof and Midge Ure. The single entered the charts at number one, stayed in that position for five whole festive weeks, and went on to sell over 3 million copies.

Other wintry wonders worthy of mention are "Merry Xmas Everybody" by Slade, which sold a quarter of a million on its first day of release and entered the UK chart every year from 1981 to 1986; "I Wish It Could Be Christmas Every Day" from Roy Wood's Wizzard; and "Last Christmas" by Wham, which was held off the number-one spot by Band Aid's offering, and after being turned into a double-A side became one of the last, UK-based, million-selling singles.

ABOVE: **Bing Crosby and Danny Kaye in a scene from the film *White Christmas*.**

OPPOSITE: **Seventies superstars Slade, whose "Merry Xmas Everybody" sold a quarter of a million copies on the first day of release.**

· YES ·

ABOVE: **A Yes album, based on obscure
Shastric scriptures, became the first to
qualify for a gold disc on ship-out sales alone.**

By any standards, the seventies were a strange decade, a time of surrealistically warped futurism, when fashion went off on flared tangents and musical directions slipped and slid between stadium-sized excess and back-to-the-roots rocking.

One of the weirdest paths ever taken by rock music was that of the so-called "progressive" rock bands, of which the most ludicrously perfect example could be found in the shape of Yes. With the clear falsetto fragility of Jon Anderson, the powerhouse pummelling of skin-basher supreme Alan White, the bombastic bass barrage of Chris Squire and the meanderingly expressive string-pinging of lanky-haired Steve Howe, Yes were the epitome of English college rock.

The group effortlessly constructed a series of pretentious and deeply meaningless rock albums; the best example of their "art" can be found in the 1973 double album *Tales From Topographic Oceans*. Allegedly based on the Shastric scriptures, it became the first album to qualify for a gold disc on ship-out sales alone.

ZEITGEIST

eitgeist is a characteristically German compound noun meaning "the spirit of the age". Its status as a compound noun means Zeitgeist has no one-word equivalent in English and as such, it is the perfect word for our purposes, not least because the connections between popular music and certain shifts in culture and history over the last half of the twentieth century have spawned, at various times, definite, palpable evocations of era and epoch.

From its earliest days as a music reflecting the hedonistic leanings of a youthful generation, eager to break free of the morality and values imposed upon them by the older generation, rock was closely allied to the lifestyles and images of its idolized inventors. The overt glamour and sexuality of Little Richard and Elvis Presley, together with the wit and innuendo of Chuck Berry, brought the secret language and encoded practices of the jazz and beat scenes to a wider and even younger audience. The new music, and the attitudes which it engendered, simultaneously stimulated and fed off a growing sense of outrage and incomprehension on the part of the parent generation.

The emergence of The Beatles coincided with a European consumer boom in the 1960s, when the post-war babies grew up to find the Western economies shaking off the deadweight of wartime austerity and finally enjoying the fruits of 20 years of peace. As well as providing a soundtrack to the prevalent atmosphere of change and positivity, the Beatles, the Stones, Bob Dylan and countless others helped to define a particular Zeitgeist in changing the image of the pop musician from slick-haired matinée idol to musician with a hitherto undiscovered degree of wit, intelligence and inventiveness. This approach helped to give credence to their attempts to make rock music something more than just ephemeral, disposable fun.

The spirit of the times has never been more closely allied to rock music than in the brief but beautiful

ABOVE LEFT: **As sixties clothes come back into fashion (witness Lenny Kravitz and Dee-Lite), these teenagers from 1968 become harder to place in time.**

ABOVE: **Musical style is only one indicator of popular change. Graphic design is also an effective marker of evolving tastes and fashions, as a comparison between an ethereal sixties festival poster and a brutally simple Who poster from just five years later shows.**

flowering of the Summer of Love in 1967. Events around the San Francisco Bay, such as the early Trips Festival allied to the writings of "The Merry Pranksters", provided a focus for the emergent, drug-based psychedelic movement. With their belief in the consciousness-expanding properties of certain hallucinogens, the flower children pushed the boundaries of music and its means of presentation, with rock gigs taking on the aura of A Consciousness Expanding Event, rather than appearing as simply a bunch of guys with guitars playing a set of songs.

Music depends upon technology for its distribution, and with the advent of conveniently usable multi-track recording techniques, John Lennon's mid-sixties dream of writing a song on Monday, recording it on Tuesday and seeing it in the shops by Friday became a realizable goal. "The Ballad of John and Yoko", which, although credited to The Beatles, featured just John and Paul and none of the other members of the band, was the first record to be made on this basis. It went to number one in the UK in 1969 and reflected the constant attention

paid by the press to the hapless Beatle in his attempts to marry his lover Yoko Ono. The technique was used yet again for "Give Peace a Chance". Recorded in a hotel room in Toronto during one of John and Yoko's "Bed-In" publicity campaigns, the song went on to become a peace anthem all over the world and provided a focus for the growing demonstrations against the US involvement in the Vietnam War. The prevailing Zeitgeist was undeniably distilled into a three-minute rock anthem.

Other examples of rock music's ability to crystalize and articulate a prevalent mood or feeling abound in the recent history of the Western world. The events which were to become known as the Punk Explosion in the UK in 1976 were as much a pointer to the times as any number of sociological reports.

Equally, in contemporary terms in the US, the continuing success and appeal of rap acts highlight a growing tendency for acts to "cross over" into mainstream chart action, building on the gradual integration of audiences, while exposing the remaining traces of

institutionalized racism. In this case, as in others, music reflects the time from which it comes and the needs of the increasingly global culture from which it springs. It is significant, therefore, that the radical voice of black America should have found a such a platform from which to address the pertinent issues in the late eighties.

Zeitgeists do not set records in themselves, but the proven ability of music of all kinds to respond to, reflect and even shape certain aspects of cultural life, demonstrates the importance of this particular means of expression to the world. When more than 200,000 people gathered to watch Roger Waters' most ambitious performance of his epic "The Wall" in July 1990 after the destruction of the Berlin Wall, the live telecast to the world helped to underline and to capture the beginning of a what has been heralded as new epoch in world politics. Whether or not such an epoch is under way, the point of change has been fixed in time and memory with the aid of rock 'n' roll.

LEFT: **Breakdancing was just one manifestation of the rap and go-go explosion in Black America in the mid eighties.**

BELOW: **The eighties was the decade for** **charity concerts and caring rock stars. There was Amnesty International's roving worldwide tour, Live Aid and Farm Aid, a concert held in Austin, Texas, organized by Willie Nelson.**

Christened Francis Vincent Zappa shortly after his birth in 1940, Frank Zappa arrived at what in some ways was to become his spiritual home of California and went to school there with a man destined to find fame as Captain Beefheart, Don Van Vliet. Not surprisingly, the two geniuses formed a band together.

One of Zappa's earliest successes came with the doo-wop classic "Memories of El Monte" in 1962, but from then on things got a little weird. With money gained from B-movie score writing, Zappa set up his own Studio Z in 1963, using the world's first and only five-track recording machine built for him by a friend. Things went smoothly for Frank for a couple of years until he was jailed on obscenity charges for 10 days. After he emerged from prison he formed The Mothers and signed to Verve Records in 1966.

Never one to toe the musical line, Zappa delighted in creating musical collages and soundscapes, satirizing the whims and fancies of crowds and performers alike while creating a musical repertoire of sometimes striking originality. For example, his 1968 release *We're Only In It For The Money* parodied The Beatles' *Sergeant Pepper* sleeve and roundly pooh-poohed the psychedelic explosion of that era.

Zappa's reputation for swimming against the tide was reinforced with every subsequent album release. The next, *Cruisin' With Ruben and the Jets*, paid homage to doo-wop while the rest of the world was picking up the sitar. The setting-up of his own Bizzarre/Straight Records meant that Zappa needed no sanction from record company bosses to secure the release of his material. *Hot Rats*, *Burnt Weeny Sandwich* and the disturbingly sleeved *Weasels Ripped My Flesh* continued Frank's characterization as an avant garde performer and rock satirist.

In 1971, Zappa became the only star whose lyrics the Royal Philharmonic declined to perform when the libretto of *200 Motels* was declared obscene. Instead Zappa made a film of the same name, featuring Ringo Starr. In spite of the satirical swipe he had taken at the band in 1968, later that same year he joined John Lennon on stage to jam, proving that in the world of rock, at least, grudges are seldom held.

Zappa's career continues today with recent releases including a mail-order-only boxed set on his own Barking Pumpkin label. But with his most recent position as a UN-sponsored cultural adviser to the newly formed Czech government under the poet Vaclav Havel, surely Zappa is the only rock 'n' roller to achieve such a lofty status while still alive.

OPPOSITE: Frank Zappa is a highly gifted composer, arranger, musician and producer, who has worked with four-piece bands and symphony orchestras.

TOP: Frank Zappa on stage with the Mothers of Invention in 1968, before being forced to cancel shows after he fell offstage in London.

ABOVE: No one looks quite like Frank Zappa, which is proved by this feeble attempt at a lookalike contest (1969)! The real McCoy lurks in the front row.

INDEX

· PICTURE CREDITS ·

All colour transparencies and black and white photographs have been supplied courtesy of Pictorial Press. Special thanks are also due to Martin Norris for providing some additional material.